To Be or Not To Be

To Be
or
Not To Be

The Question of Parenthood

Eileen Farrell

Scepter

Chicago   Dublin   London

176
FZ45

Grateful acknowledgment for permission to reprint articles in this volume is made to: *America,* the National Catholic Weekly Review, 920 Broadway, New York, for "Love, O Love, O Careful Love" and "Freedom to Die"; *The Way Magazine,* London, for "As Christ Loved the Church"; L. Michael Curtin, for "Children"; *Mundo Cristiano,* Madrid, for "How Many Children"; *Pittsburgh Catholic,* for "French Awakening"; *Commonweal,* for "The Rock Book"; *Pax Romana Journal,* Fribourg, for "The Economics of Population". Grateful acknowledgment for translations of papal documents is also made to: *The Pope Speaks,* Pius XII—"The Large Family" and John XXIII—"To the Family Front", "Feast of the Holy Family" and "Mater et Magistra"; to Rev. Edgar R. Smothers, S.J. for Paul VI—"To Large Family Association"; NCWC News Service, for Cardinal Montini's "Letter to Catholic Social Week"; John A. Gueguen, for Cardinal Montini's "Per la famiglia cristiana"; and The Daughters of St. Paul, for all other documents used. Grateful acknowledgment also to Farrar, Straus and Company, for quotation used from "Dear Newlyweds".

Contents

You stand, dear sons and daughters,
before the Creator,
chosen to prepare His ways.

For it will also depend on you
whether those souls will cross
the threshold of life
whom Love desires to call
from nothingness
to make them His elect. . .

Or whether they will remain
magnificent divine ideas
quenched
by the indifference or selfishness
of men.

Pius XII

FOREWORD

In October 1963 *America,* the national Catholic weekly, carried an article which is one of the reprints in this small but significant book. I found the article as refreshing as are the unexpected East winds that occasionally bring relief from the oppressive, humid heat that sometimes smothers New England in August. Jane Hanover Adams' reflections had just such an effect on me, as one of the millions who are unable to find a current magazine on the news stands which does not carry as one of its principal features another rehash of the incessant presentation of the case for contraception, the need for "Catholic" contraception, new methods of "pluralistic" contraception and/or the economic, social, moral, psychiatric, political, military and educational advantages of contraception.

In recent months that bombardment of propaganda in behalf of contraception has been not only intensified but all but infinite in its variety. The propaganda has, however, been under way for a long time and its effects have long been clear. Jane Hanover Adams' protest in *America* brought back the memory of one of the first occasions when I began to perceive, with sickening clarity, how effective the propaganda has proved even back in 1949.

A balanced, healthy Christian woman, whose normally sanguine temperament had made it possible for her to combine happily the vocation of a mother with a singularly active career in the community, had been giving some of the lectures in a course of preparation for marriage for a group of young women. She wrote me to say that she would not be available for a course the following year or thereafter. "I might as well level with you," she said. "These girls are creeps. I am old enough to be their grandmother, but I find their whole view of life and of themselves too depressing for me. They have been so conditioned by the women's magazines, by some of their professors and by the dismal smog of the birth control propaganda that all that seems to interest them enough to ask questions about it is bound up with birth pains, the effect of pregnancy on any unsuspected heart conditions, the ideal limit of children for a wife who plans to keep up her travel interests, and similar calculations that preoccupy them far more than meeting with them interests me. I hate to say it, but although a number of them are attractive enough and still bear signs of being reclaimable if a good doctor and a capable husband can take them over in time, I look upon them as bleak prospects for marriage. I'm afraid that nothing I can tell them out of my memories has any meaning for them. I was a wife and a mother, not a clinical psychiatrist nor a sociologist. I had my problems and still have. These girls do not *have* problems; they *are* problems—and the planned parenthood propaganda has done more than anything else to make them such. If patient men can make women of some of them, they are welcome. Maybe later, when troubles really hit them, I'd like to talk these over with them. But right now I suspect them of frigidity induced by egoism and a mania for cold, convenient security."

Remembering the sobering reflections of that day, I was perhaps excessively grateful for Jane Hanover Adams' article. But even remembering this, I was unprepared for some of the first reactions to the *America* piece that came my way. I shall not soon forget the sneer that formed on the lips of a fairly representative young intellectual to whom I handed the article for quick reading. I had seen that sneer before on other lips; I have seen it many times at discussions of what is increasingly referred to as the "fertility cult" alleged to typify Catholics, including, thank God, Catholic intellectuals. The sneer has become, for me, one of the most disturbing symptoms of the attitude that Father de Lestapis calls "the contraceptive mentality."

Hence the timeliness of the publication within a single set of covers of the reflections and reprints brought together in this book. It is a small little pebble indeed for the slingshot with which the David of those who remember the wonders of generous parenthood must meet the Goliath of the calculators backed by foundation funds, newspapers, Government bureaus and all the increasing pressure groups of the contraceptionists. But it is at least a symbol that gives one increased confidence that not all the moral idealism and sturdy love for which Jane Hanover Adams spoke up will be destroyed by the slick slogans of those who sneer at the Christian tradition as having hitherto presented "merely biological, not to say zoological concepts of sex and parenthood." It is a reminder of the perennial values to which even the new slogans pay tribute when they speak, with whatever purpose, of "voluntary maternity" and "planned parenthood," well knowing that the positive appeal of these nouns is more powerful in millions of hearts than the negations that a contraceptive civilization tries to hide within the adjectives.

✠ John Wright
Bishop of Pittsburgh

Part One

I

To Being

The title of this volume is a salute to a favorite author who, despite being 400, seems to be getting more relevant all the time. Late 20th Century man does not wish "to grunt and sweat under a weary life" any more than early 17th Century man did. But modern man's formula for avoiding "the heartaches and the thousand natural shocks that flesh is heir to" is to have few heirs. And to him, King Lear's curse-of-curses sounds more like an earnest supplication, "a consummation," so to speak, "devoutly to be wished,":

> Hear, nature! hear, dear goddess, hear!
> Suspend thy purpose, if thou didst intend
> To make this creature fruitful!
> Into her womb convey sterility!
> Dry up in her the organs of increase;
> And from her derogate body never spring
> A babe to honor her!

* * *

Some while ago I was persuaded by the dearest and best of men to enter matrimony. Having grown, in due time and thanks to the patience of all concerned, into motherhood, I like to ponder sometimes about the goods of family life.

What warms me when I think about our family is, I am sure, just what warms all other addicts who always and everywhere have succumbed to the business of new life. It is compounded of an incurable sense of wonder; of many kinds of bearing; of learning how lives are woven together; of forgetting about debits and credits in the book of love.

For some people there can also be a concern for what is helpful to families in general. In our case this led to participation in the Cana movement in its young days, to much reading and thought and observation and discussion of the norms of Catholic family life.

We got married three years after Pius XII became the servant of the servants of God. And so we began fulfilling the primary and secondary ends of marriage during those new-springtime years when the Mystical Body was pulsing with the inspiration and teaching and prayer of one whom history should know as the Pope of the Family. I do not doubt that the effect of his fatherly care reached into our home. And his apostolic blessing, in Our Lord, must have descended there often through the ministry of loved and loving priests who came to our hearthfire.

I think I first knew how penetrating both his love and his understanding were when the Allocution to the Midwives reached us in 1951. From then on, everything he said about marriage and family was like a letter from home. He died, but the letters kept coming. For John, with his great fatherly heart, let it be known that the theme of the family was especially dear to him, one of a family of ten himself; and he spoke of the "holy joy that stirs in a family every time a man is born into the world."

Nor did the communication cease when he left us, for now it is Paul who speaks - and he speaks of protecting the family in all that concerns the exercise of its high function. When he lately reminded us that the Church and the Papacy are supposed to *love* one another, I found it a big hardship not to be able to dial direct and tell him, "Holy Father, we *do!*"

This brief synopsis of my ongoing interpersonal relationship with Rome may help to explain what is done to me when some of my siblings in the household of the faith decide to ignore our father, ("After all, he was an *old* man when he said that!" . . . "After all, he *has* to take a conservative stance!"); or to disparage his wisdom and vision; or to keep raising the question of what teachings are *really* infallible. Prescinding from whatever may be proper for the theologian in his professional capacity, I have thought that whether this criticism comes from the archconservative, explicitly rejecting the magistra of *Mater et Magistra* or from the ultraliberal who actually rejects both in his efforts to conform the Church to secular values, the querulous, adolescent tone prevails.

I don't know how many times the "mutual love" error has to be brought out of the mothballs, or Margaret Sanger's approach to non-life refurbished and served up as the latest thinking-in-depth on the family-in-the-modern-world. But I have a natural inclination toward grandparenthood and if certain people, including professors, theologians, reluctant mothers, and all the rest, don't lay off, there might not be anyone around one of these years but us senior citizens.

Such thoughts as these led to the writing of "Love, O Love, O Careful Love." In no way was it intended to be a reflection on those good parents who are inhibited from accepting God's gift

3

of children at some point in their lives, and who have problems enough as it is. Rather its thrust was in the direction of the anti-child neurosis of our times and those who (I trust unthinkingly) cultivate in others a fear of fruitfulness. I was more narrator than author because I really only draped the fabric of many conversations over the framework of my own knowledge. For this and other reasons, I used a pseudonym.

After "Love, O Love" appeared in *America,* I began to get letters from near and far, from other parents, from priests, from religious. It became plain that there was concern everywhere over the campaign against the fruitfulness of marriage, which is consequently a campaign against the vocation of marriage. Each letter was another beam of light, not meant to be hidden under a bushel. There were sidelights too, as for instance the practical ecumenism suggested by a letter from Sweden, from a mother (male theologians will forgive my nominating her a Doctor of the Church), a convert who before long will be the mother of both a Lutheran minister and a Catholic priest. Ut unum sint.

It seemed that these letters should be shared, and perhaps rounded out by some other pertinent magazine articles. And then I wanted, partly in order to have these passages together in one place, and partly to make them better known and loved, to include excerpts and some complete documents from our Holy Fathers. Even those which are not "official" pronouncements can serve to clarify points, for they bear witness to those truths which a loving Mother has always taught us. They are, in the truest sense, the words of life!

4

II

Love, O Love O Careful Love

Our daughter was recently being catechized on the sacraments, in preparation for confirmation. Having grown accustomed, though reluctantly, to hearing the "new thinking" on marriage expounded far and wide, I half expected an analysis of "family planning" in the text. Hence I was enormously pleased to find a simple and stately exposition of the family, including such traditional thoughts as: "Parents must work and sacrifice together to provide for the spiritual and physical needs of their family," and "If they keep God's law in their marriage, they can depend upon God to give them the graces they need to fulfill the purpose of their marriage." This latter, our daughter was able to tell me, is "to continue the human race."

I fear that she has encountered such straightforward, uncomplicated teaching about her possible future vocation for about the last time, and that when she takes up the subject again, later, she will find it cloaked in enough clauses, conditions and concern to confuse even the subtlest mind.

If she attends one of our Catholic high schools, she will presently take a course on marriage. For the most part I envy her this opportunity. Though the discussion of canon law, impediments and divorce may not just fascinate her, there will come

5

some commonsense talk about dating, to augment the running dialogue at home. There will be, I know, inspiration and motivation, and, in the main, a thoroughly Christian perspective on that vocation of love and generosity and service which is marriage. Whether she plights her troth to a husband, whether she becomes a consecrated virgin, or whether she stays single in the world, she needs to have this outlook, and I am grateful for the help.

But one fine morning there is likely to be an "additive" for which I will not give thanks. She will hear—from a priest, a doctor, a married couple (perhaps from all of these)—that even though children *are* the primary purpose of marriage, there are some important whereases in the contract. A truly prudent married couple, it will be explained, expects to space and limit their offspring judiciously so as not to overproduce. They must do this in a morally permissible way, of course, as God expects them to; and "control" is the password.

She may even be advised to start compiling a record that will enable her to keep an eagle eye on her cycle at all times (though by then a urine or saliva test may make the whole process simpler, if more clinical), and so accomplish prudent reproduction. But whatever the current "how to," it will be presented on the theory that she will eventually practice family limitation if she marries, and that this is the way to keep her safe from the evils of contraception. (Meanwhile, if certain proposals are adopted, the man-to-be in her future may even be getting drilled in conditioning his reproductive reflexes.)

I well know that in a public high school she could encounter a "life adjustment" course instead, and learn about self-expression and feminine fulfillment and the contraceptive way. I know, too, that there is agitation to introduce the subject at the fifth-grade level.

But in either case, and even if the matter were ignored academically as of old, other teachers wait anxiously in the wings. For instance, she can pick up Catholic periodicals around the house, at the doctor's or dentist's office or at church, and find articles, sometimes interspersed with related advertisements, on "responsible parenthood." There will likely be a ban-the-babies piece by a lay or professional person, or by a priest in sociology or demography; or a survey in which married couples reveal bitterness about their fecundity and the Church's intransigence; or the after-thoughts of a middle-ager who perhaps took a fling at large-family life during the heady days of the 1940's and 1950's and is now ready to concede. (Were the neighbors and the in-laws right after all?)

Editors who surely would blanch at the thought of exposing a mentally sick priest to public view will no doubt still be filling their columns with case histories of disturbed mothers (as a warning to the foolhardy) and illustrations worthy of the Neo-Malthusian League. Not to mention an occasional series in the secular press by someone, Catholic or otherwise, who: a) agrees with the birth-control movement in everything but the *means*, and is able to quote one or more responsible theologians to support his position, or b) agrees with the birth-control movement and considers it only a matter of time and patient understanding on both sides until the Church, pushed forward by an aroused laity, catches up with the 20th century.

Another eager teacher may be right in the parish, in the person of the occasional curate who works with the teen-agers—who is rightly a hero and mentor to them, and who is "nervous about large families.

At this point, it would be unnatural indeed if she didn't begin to wonder about her parents and whether she and her brothers were "the effect of blind passion or the fruit of nature's unknown whim" (as one writer expresses it), or whether, since our family is not a large one, they were the result of prudent planning. She may begin to wonder, also, considering the more densely populated homes of some of her friends, if their parents have the "rabbit-warren morality" referred to by yet another Catholic spokesman, or whether they just hadn't heard that whereas "formerly the problem had to be left to Divine Providence," there was now "a new dimension in Catholic family thinking." (We'll have news for her on these points—one item of which will be that if you're looking for libertines, don't waste your time on the parents of numerous children. Even Margaret Sanger recognized that *one* marital act a year "might be sufficient to keep a woman with one child in her womb and another at her breast during her entire childbearing period.")

Then college, if she goes. We're rather glad that worries about the expense of college didn't interfere with *her* advent into the world. If she wants and can make college and we can't afford an expensive one, there are excellent "streetcar" colleges in our city—scholarships and student-aid plans for the deserving, too. College can somewhat enlarge her knowledge of the new thinking, though the young rebels who used to say (and mean): "No church is going to tell *me* how many children to have," will have turned to other quarrels because it will seem evident that this battle has long since been won.

We hope she will be stimulated to learn about the social teachings of the Church; but we predict she may very well hear all about *Mater et Magistra,* for instance, *except* those embarrasing passages on Providence and population. (How else explain the almost simultaneous appearance of an article urging students to take up this encyclical and a hearty endorsement, by the same writer, of Dr. Rock's book?) She may also learn to quote verbatim Pius XII's three well-worn sentences about the hoped-for refinement of the licit method for regulating offspring, and remain ignorant of the literally thousands of eloquent sentences he spoke on the blessing of offspring and the significance to Christianity of the large family.

Perhaps in time this girl of ours will choose marriage. Well, then, a refresher course on "responsible parenthood" may be included in her preparation for the sacrament of matrimony. At her nuptials, incidentally, the Church will pray that she may be "rich in children," but I suppose that's just the vestigial remains of an ancient agrarian society, utterly irrelevant to modern life. Still later, she and her husband can review the whole subject and its "mystique" at a renewal day for young married people. Very possibly a book will be recommended that paints a beautiful picture of married love, only to destroy it by recommending a compensatory sexual practice, which readers of Aldous Huxley will recognize as the exquisitely pleasurable yoga of love practiced by the most enlightened inhabitants of the "Island."

All in all, I wonder if our girl will stand a chance of approaching her vocation in the frame of mind and heart befitting a Christian bride—not so much because of pressures from a hostile and worldly society, but because the very guides she has reason to trust will unwittingly have handicapped her. Throughout this time, of course, we parents will not be sitting idly by. But we

9

wish conditions were not being systematically set up that can only make it more difficult for young Christians to approach the maturity asked of them by the Sermon on the Mount.

The kind of responsibility we should like our daughter to acquire is a loving response to a loving Father who speaks to her through the people and the circumstances of her life, a humble and "resolute willingness to undergo inevitable fatigue and sacrifices in the fulfillment of a mission so noble and often so arduous as is the co-operation with God in the transmission of human life and the education of offspring" (*Mater et Magistra,* § 195).

We think she should develop a great respect—an awe, really—for the vocation of marriage, be sure it is *her* vocation, and then be ready to give herself to it with courage and good cheer, instead of foolishly standing on her fictitious rights against her own God, fighting the very love that is meant to make her into a fully developed human being.

The kind of prudence we would see grow in her is not the anxiety of the fainthearted, the apprehensive caution of the fearful. In the words of Father Gerald Vann:

> One might suppose that our Lord had said He had come not that we mght have life but that we might have safety. And therefore prudence has come to mean, quite simply, caution, the caution necessary to avoid all danger and ensure complete safety. To such an extent has the greatest of the cardinal virtues come down in the world.

Prudence about marriage, for her, ought to mean a prudent decision to marry or not to marry, when to marry, whom to marry. If she is unable to exercise prudence on these questions, which will directly affect numerous lives, then a future decision to "plan" will likely not be the sudden blooming of prudence, but caution masquerading as prudence. Let her rather take counsel and be wise in her choice of vocation and preparation for it, and then let her live it with a stout heart.

The kind of control she ought to cultivate is chastity—that of the virgin while she is unmarried, that of the wife if she marries. Such control would rule out her yielding to intemperate desire either through fornication or through contracting marriage too early. (In marriage, it might be added, this would not only rule out adultery, but also the touch of Jansenism which counts it somehow more godly for married people to eschew the marital act, or the touch of hedonism which implies that there really isn't anything much else.)

I cannot understand why anyone would want her to think that control in marriage is a matter of successfully avoiding "too many babies," or that temperance can be acquired by deliberately sowing the seed of life on barren ground. Or that periodic continence is not merely a remedy for medical, social, economic and eugenic ills, but is, in fact, the "prudent" way of married life. Or that, anyhow, given the conditions of modern life, she will inevitably have one or more of the licit reasons for family limitation. Or that babies (after the first four at least) may somehow be an evil to be avoided instead of a gift to be cherished. Or that family limitation does not exact a stiff toll in moral, psychological and spiritual problems. Or that every couple will produce an excessive number of children unless controlled—when in fact sterility, complete or partial, is a major medical problem. Or indeed that any thinking couple must view with alarm the fast multiplying world population and decide whether they have the right to add even one new hungry mouth (in our overfed country).

At an age when her idealism is at a peak, her mind alert, her capacities growing, she will be receptive to the words of life. Should she not hear them, instead of the dismal predictions of those who tremble at the thought of more human life? Will there be someone to call forth a joyful echo in her heart with words like these from Pope Paul:

Efforts to re-establish the equilibrium between growing population and means of livelihood are therefore not to be directed toward violation of the laws of life or interference with the natural flux and flow of the human family. Such an attitude of renouncement of life, indeed, kills the noblest aspirations of the spirit; while a declining birth rate, aimed at by such systems, has always proved sooner or later to be, in the history of the nations, a sign of defeat and of doom.

We want her to see the dignity of Christian marriage, to consider soberly, but not morbidly, the gamut of possibilities implicit in the marriage vows. We want her to have confidence in her innate ability to cope and to hope, to meet difficulties with composure instead of panic.

Nature has equipped her to receive and carry and nourish the gift of new life. Her heart will grow to embrace her spouse and the whole harvest of their love—if she is not conditioned to reject them. The grace of matrimony, perfecting nature's gifts, can fashion her into a wise and inwardly tranquil wife and mother whose best contribution to Church and State is good sons and daughters—their number now hidden in the inscrutable mystery of God's creative love.

If there are those who would assist us as we try to prepare this girl for her life, if they would earn our gratitude, let them try to apprehend the mysterious making of the family as its natural and supernatural destiny unfolds; reverently study the norms implanted in nature by God; resist all temptations to reduce marriage and family to a mechanical formula acceptable to human wisdom. Granted this approach, we think a certain husband-to-be, if he exists, may one day have cause to be grateful, too.

As for now, we hope she will always remember that the Vicar of Christ who reigned in Rome in the year of her confirmation said: "Don't be afraid of the numbers of your sons and daughters. On the contrary, ask Providence for them so that you can rear and educate them to their benefit and to the glory of your fatherland here on earth, and of that in heaven." And again: "Every night I say the third decade of the rosary for all the babies born in the last 24 hours, because they are the treasure of the future." And, in his last letter to the Roncalli family: "Oh, the children, what a richness the children are, what a blessing!"

III

Angels and Ministers of Grace

Soon there were pleasant additions to the daily mail. A college president wrote that the article would be recommended reading for her student body. A theology teacher reported using it for a classroom discussion topic. A truly fatherly Monsignor who does not ordinarily write to authors, wanted to assure me that when the inevitable criticism started, I could count on "at least one enthusiastic rooter."

A Cardinal wrote from Rome that he had enjoyed the article and found it a "worthwhile contribution to this complicated discussion." A Bishop subsequently wrote, "I was at the Council when it appeared. It was like a breath of clean fresh air in the midst of a smog—not in Rome but in the magazine world. I do not mind confessing that I was moved to tears."

Here are some of the letters:

Dear Mrs. Adams:

I cannot imagine how you have such an insight into this subject. According to your article you do not have a large family. Yet each line, each paragraph seems to me the true way all parents should feel about their children who have the vocation of marriage.

I have a large family. All through the thirty years of my married life I have been criticized. God in many, many ways gave me the assurance that I was following His will. But nowhere else did I find the same assurance. We were married during the depression when having a baby was almost unheard of. Then during the war we were accused of avoiding the draft. After the war we were told by many that we should practice more self control. And now, having a large family raises the taxes or creates a population explosion!

But within our home how different it all is. My husband and I love and respect each other more than anyone else I have ever known. Our children love each other and look forward to seeing their married brothers and sisters, nephews and nieces. In turn, our married children look forward to coming home as one of the greatest events in their life.

We chose Thanksgiving Day as our family reunion day. It isn't possible for anyone to know the pleasure and happiness both my husband and I experience on this day. Last year our children, our married children and their husbands and wives, and our ten grandchildren were all here with us. Our joy on this day was truly indescribable.

We have both reached the age of fifty-two. We still have seven at home, the youngest one being seven. Whatever time God is still going to grant us, we are looking forward to enjoying. I know there are many happy events to come; also sorrows along the way which I do not fear as God has never failed us.

Please accept my sincere gratitude. I shall pray that God will reward you for the comfort you brought to me from your article. I know it will assist my girls too, and I hope *they* won't have the *one cloud* that hung over our entire married life.

Mrs. Henry J. Read
Patchogue, N. Y.

Dear Mrs. Adams:

As a former professor of Pastoral Theology, I have given a great deal of thought to this subject. A priest would need a heart of stone not to sympathize with many individual heart-rending situations. Yet I agree completely with your implied thesis that the emphasis is now being put in the wrong place. Such a statement was long overdue.

> Msgr. Edgar P. McCarren
> Rockville Centre, N. Y.

* * *

Dear Mrs. Adams:

Many modern writers see only a need to combat the world population problem and try to meet the problem by creating a desire to limit family size. They then go into lengthy discussions of the licit and illicit means of limitation. It is indeed a novel and refreshing article that skips the social trauma of choosing the means of regulation and goes to the heart of the matter, "the blessing of children."

> Ronald Burke
> Notre Dame, Ind.

* * *

Dear Mrs. Adams:

It is most encouraging, in all this melee of conflicting opinions on family life, parenthood and public policy, to read a statement so firm, so calm, so well-developed, so fully Christian. It is four-square, as not all our Catholic treatments of the subject are, with the most highly authorized pastoral teaching we have; and it has its own special authority because a wife and mother has written it.

I count it with the statement by Fathers Ford and Kelly of

the moral theology of marriage relations, in the *Catholic World* (October, 1963), and Dr. Ratner's forceful assertion of sound medical doctrine in *The Commonweal* (July 5, 1963) as an important element in our counter-offensive not only against the avowed promoters of the whole contraceptive program, but against the writers who exploit differences among Catholics on the subject, or who carry their irenic concern for our separated brethren so far as seriously to obscure the issue. What is needed is a moderate, balanced judgment and a due concern to harmonize and not to divide Catholics in our common front against the world, the flesh and the devil.

The demographic argument seems to me very doubtfully in place when it is brought to bear on the right and responsibility of husband and wife with regard to their own family. If they remain within the bounds of honest prudence, so far as the common good of the domestic society is concerned, by that fact they will fulfill their whole duty to society at large. And God will bless them for a generous trust in Him.

We do need the voice of our pastors sounding loud and clear. It is for this I hope and pray, above all for the sake of our Catholic people who suffer in this state of muddled uncertainty. We are not accustomed to live through such a far-reaching crisis in doctrine and in way of life; and we need great patience and trust in God. They will have their reward.

The whole matter of birth-control, which has been so much agitated in recent years, seems to mount from climax to climax. I hope and pray that we may have before long, from the Council or from the Holy Father, a full, luminous reaffirmation of sound doctrine on this subject.

A Priest of the Society of Jesus

Dear Mrs. Adams:

"Love, O Love" is like a cool drink of water. The positive approach has psychological benefits that are seldom taken into account!

Mrs. George Clark
Columbus, Ohio

*   *   *

Dear Mrs. Adams:

When all Catholics forget about the population explosion and concentrate on what sex and marriage are for, they will come back to thinking with the Church. In every society where chastity is the rule, the incidental problems, like overcrowding, will be taken care of, for such a society will be regulated by Catholic thinking which meets all difficulties without breaking the Catholic whole, the holos.

The Church can have no attraction for the world unless it is presented as a Whole consistent in all its parts, remaining the same from one age to the next. If the magisterium is treated as just one voice among many competing for assent, to be disregarded in favor of one that is more "up-to-date", what attraction can it have for anybody? To quote Hermann Bahr, an Austrian who left the Church and then returned to it: "A Church which regards itself, so to speak, as one among many variants of a text can offer me no certitude; and of uncertainties I have quite enough of my own."

Paul Hallett
Denver, Col.

*   *   *

Dear Mrs. Adams:

It is a relief to know there are women capable of intelligently

18

and realistically expressing God's way of life. Our eager young Christians seem to be finding confusion along the way. Those with a little more experience must be the steady lamps shining for them. Then they can see that God's standards of peace and love can be achieved, despite challenges and struggles, and that the end result is always Joy!

Sister Mary Jennings, R.C.
Carmichael, Cal.

*　　*　　*

Dear Mrs. Adams:

In my circle of friends, I keep trying to push the following of God's will in our daily lives, which naturally includes the number of children one is liable to have. Most of my friends could well afford any number of children, but I guess the personal sacrifice is a bit too much. I hear every excuse but the real one. And when we get onto the population explosion, my voice is lost in the tumult.

I guess I shouldn't judge, and I don't say too much because one can lose one's influence. That's why your article pleased me. It said all the things I wish I could say to my friends in a clear, well-informed manner. Don't give up! Your words will be heard and perhaps some will give them serious thought.

Mrs. M. J. Healy
Chicago, Ill.

*　　*　　*

Dear Mrs. Adams:

I have circulated copies of your article among persons of influence here. I also hope some day to translate it into Japanese.

I believe that few of those who speak of exporting rhythm to overpopulated nations as a means of solving overpopulation really know the score. When these people are advanced far enough up the economic and social ladder to want to, and be able to follow the rhythm method, there will be no need for advice on this score from Catholics in the U.S. Before that time, it will only confuse the people and encourage much worse actions on the part of governments, like the drive for mass sterilization in India.

Rev. Anthony Zimmerman, SVD
Gifu Ken, Japan

Dear Mrs. Adams:

I have been waiting and hoping for just such an eloquent cry from a Christian parent bespeaking the spiritual vision of marriage and love of children. It is so much needed as antidote to the uninspired emphasis on techniques and numbers and the primacy of the economic.

You quote and you echo the clear teaching of the Church at the highest level—a teaching too casually dismissed by many who are immersed in research statistics.

Neither you nor I would wish to disdain any of the developing knowledge which God's Providence may provide for the help of parents in a sacramental vocation. But you are right to insist on the values that are deeper still, always enduring and ever primary—the vision of God's love and care, the generosity of persons committed to love and reverence for human life.

I share your unease with much that is written in the present Catholic debate. May God give energy and resonance in the debate to voices like yours.

Rev. Paul J. Murphy, S.J.
Boston, Mass.

Dear Mrs. Adams:

Let anyone say what he will, all this population explosion talk is telling God that He has erred in not diminishing the rate of human fecundity in accord with modern opinion and difficulties of the present day—as though famines and other hardships never had happened before—and that it is for us to correct His rash creative impulses.

Granted that God wills the creation of souls only conditionally —if He has human cooperation—but when that is given *then* He takes over and freely wills existence or non-existence of a soul.

God is never compelled to create, nor does He do it carelessly. He does not lump so many tens of millions of souls to be created this year. Each one is a special selection out of all possibilities and with full foreknowledge of just what will be the advantages and disadvantages, the happiness and the troubles. Who is any one of us to tell Him that in this particular case, we know better what should be done and will exercise our veto, so depriving Him of any say in the matter?

A confessor may not be more strict than the Church, and to prevent a greater evil undoubtedly should refer some penitents to a Catholic physician, but even this is perilous. As a professor of surgery told his class, "There are indications for an operation and there are opportunities for an operation."

On another plane, what effect does it have on conjugal love deliberately to rule out God and accept a secular motive? It does not show immediately, but in the long run? Another point, do you know of any family which wants education but which cannot get it? There are few families regardless of size, that do not have as good or better education than their parents.

God most certainly has built up this nation for a great work.

In less than two centuries we have come up from a mainly empty wilderness to the leading nation of the world. With our new luxury and ease perhaps we will have to be toughened by some more hard going before we really settle down.

Rt. Rev. Msgr. H. D. Buchanan
El Paso, Texas

Dear Mrs. Adams:

Talk about Divine Providence! I was reading through some reprints from a Catholic magazine on marriage, the pill, overpopulation, etc., and getting more and more annoyed at this panicky attitude on the part of some writers. Then I read your article and suddenly the world was back in God's love. This is truly a great contribution, an affirmation from one who believes and hence can love.

Rev. Raymond Smith, O.P.
Dover, Mass.

* * *

Dear Mrs. Adams:

Let me tell you about some lovely, inspiring friends of mine who evidently aren't tempted to try contraception:

One has nine children between the ages of 3 and 16 years. Although limited bedroom space forces her to put her five girls into one bedroom, she told me she'd love to have another baby.

Another friend in a 3-bedroom house has seven children. Her mother lives with them too.

Last year another friend and her husband gave up their bedroom to the children and took the living room couch for their bed. That was before their 7th child was born.

Another lost her 12th child at birth. When she had her 13th child it was warmly received.

Another had her 10th child a year and a half ago. Her house is attractive and well cared for, but definitely on the small side. She, too, is expecting.

I know women, and you do, too, with far fewer children who, when you mention "the next one" to them, throw up their hands and cry, "Oh no! Not for me. I've had my share!" But not these lovely ladies. Why? What do these five have in common besides ear plugs and an ignorance of the "beauty" of contraception? They breast feed their babies!

Are they rebellious at the thought of another child? Do they cry out, "No, we can't afford another!" or "No, we haven't room for another!" or "No, my nerves can't take it!"? They have every right to. I am confident, however, they just smile and quietly say, "There's always room for one more."

Why do they think differently from so many others who seek the safety of contraceptives, oral or otherwise? Why do they have a "we'll-manage-somehow" philosophy regarding one more child? Do you suppose mysterious influences are exerted on the mother who breast feeds, nurturing within her tranquility and confidence, both in God and in man? Do you suppose that is why these good women can warmly embrace another child when the house is already bulging?

Don't you see, these friends don't need contraceptives to protect them from unwanted babies, for they don't have unwanted babies!

This may sound corny, but we mothers need no pill to protect us from unwanted babies. All we need is the sugar-coating on

23

the medication which God prescribed for a wholesome, happy marriage. The medication is babies. The sugar-coating, the breast, is a combination of medically-proven active ingredients —and oh, *so* habit-forming! And that, Mrs. Adams, is the secret! Once a woman has nursed successfully, she'd never have a contraceptive in the house. She'd have no need of one!

Does a wedding band on her finger and a child in her womb for nine months automatically make a girl a great mother? Or has she yet to grow in wisdom and in grace? Is it not possible that according to God's plan some of this growing will take place during the months a mother has her child at her breast?

If you want your daughter to look upon babies as a gift to be cherished rather than an evil to be avoided, do help her look upon the subject of breast feeding in a wholesome light so if and when she does have a baby she will easily and naturally put it to her breast and reap all the benefits God intended.

> Mrs. Mary Ann Cullen
> Stamford, Conn.

*   *   *

Dear Mrs. Adams:

This is just a short note from Korea to thank you from the bottom of my heart for your very timely article. You expressed my feelings and thought on the matter very wonderfully.

Our moral theologians search for the minimum in order to find a path for the weak. But it certainly is not the ideal. I feel tremendously sorry for the poor mothers and fathers who are betraying their vocation in the name of prudence and all the other alleged reasons. They will reap the harvest of their selfish "prudence" in themselves alone. But when a priest says this, the stock answer is, "What does a celibate know about it?" A priest should know that God loves generosity and sacrifice and that there is where happiness, riches, and love are found.

Korea, thank God, is still pretty free of the birth control mind despite the efforts of the government to push it. But it will come. In the meantime I marvel and am humbled by the self-sacrifice and long suffering of most Korean mothers in rearing their many children in the poverty of Korea. And I know there are still many such generous mothers in America. I am very glad that one, at least, has spoken up and beg you to keep speaking. So many of our good Catholic parents feel on the defensive: as if they should be ashamed of wanting to have children, or as if it were idiocy or some kind of perversion. If those who have the truth, the vision and the desire for the ideal speak up, they will surely give courage to others.

Rev. R. Al Rauckhorst, M.M.
Mou Ki, Korea

*   *   *

Dear Mrs. Adams:

For the past year I have noticed the trend you mention in the article among many Catholic writers. To say the least, such a trend disturbs me. One would think there is no place left in the world for generosity and trust in God's Providence. I will make your article required reading in the two seminaries where I teach; this disturbing mentality is something I have mentioned in class quite often.

Rev. Kevin D. O'Rourke, O.P.
Dubuque, Iowa

*   *   *

Dear Mrs. Adams:

Your article was translated and distributed among the Danish

Catholic priests. One of them was so kind as to send it to me. He knew I was interested in this problem and, like you, troubled about educating our children on the point of sexual morality in a secularized world.

It was a relief and a comfort to me to find my own thoughts so clearly expressed by you, and it was encouraging to see such considerations published. It is so important to insure that secularized thoughts are not the only ones to appear.

I am a convert. My husband too had decided to convert before his death. We have six sons. Three of them are Catholic. My eldest is a clergyman in the Swedish Church. The second, who is studying in Germany, will be a Catholic priest here in Sweden.

The clear stand of the Church in moral questions was one of the reasons for my conversion. I have always considered the Catholic principles in these things as the only ones which are natural and ethical.

Of late I have felt myself isolated and my point of view declared hopelessly uncontemporary. To be uncontemporary is, I think, nearly the most unpardonable of sins today, at least here in Scandinavia.

What has troubled me most of all is the fact that one cannot even count upon support from all the clergy, in spite of the clear words of at least four popes (Pius XI, Pius XII, John XXIII, and Paul VI).

For the people of today all these popes are great authorities in social, scientific, and theological questions, and with good reason, but in a matter of such great importance for the everyday life of the greatest part of the Church, you can meet with a supercilious attitude toward the papal declarations, a kind of "I know better" mentality which causes unsteadiness and upsets instead of helping people.

Why do the priests act in this way? Are they afraid to lose the young people? Is it a sort of tactics? Whatever the reasons, this attitude is fatal for the true values of matrimony.

I think we who share the opinion expressed in your article must not tire of repeating the fundamentality of the Church's teaching, in spite of opposition from people who mean to understand the times better. The world tries to conquer and to destroy the Church in many different ways. Every age has its temptations, I believe. The people of today are so eager to adapt their behavior and conception of life to the modern standard (which is valid only incidentally) they nearly forget that a human being's destination is eternity.

Fru Inger Cavallin
Lerum, Sweden

IV

Slings and Arrows

"Most of the reactions seem to have been very fine," *America's* editor told me. "There was a disagreeing note here and there, but the predominant voice was most favorable."

Among those who disagreed, Mrs. Adams was characterized as one "out of touch with reality," as one who set up "a hodgepodge of unChristianity and plain nonsense to assure her easy literary victory."

"The struggling family with seven, eight and nine children needs help, not sermons," said one critic. "How much sense would an article like that make to a hungry woman in India with a child at her breast and another in her belly?" asked another. And, "Mrs. Adams must be extremely talented at uttering high-sounding platitudes," thought a third.

"The author mocks those who see logical objections. But she neither states nor answers those objections," said one letter. "Her greatest difficulty is sheer lack of imagination. . . To piously rant on about the glories of family living to the woman whose husband is a drunkard or unfaithful is simply stubborn, dangerous nonsense."

The article was "lyrical but hopelessly unrealistic," in the view of another writer who went on to condemn a priest who had advised married people to "abandon themselves to God's (?) plan . . . When a fertile couple continues the conjugal relationship into the fertile period, they must assume the responsibility for the resulting pregnancy and not thrust it upon God."

Those who judged the Adams point of view callous may not have seen that it involved no quarrel with periodic continence as a *remedy* when indicated and possible. The issue was the growing tendency to make family limitation, under the pseudonym of "responsible parenthood" the enlightened way of married life, and the related process by which the increasing technical knowledge of how not to conceive a child has somehow made the child no longer a natural and supernatural gift but a parasite.

If "Love, O Love" sounded unrealistic, as it did to some, or harsh and reactionary, as it did to others, this is the risk one knowingly takes in questioning a vogue. But here are two letters which it elicited and which literally overflow with the sympathy and understanding of great hearts. The writers are not oblivious of life's difficulties, nor do they judge the motives of others. Rather they are able to look calmly upon the "sea of troubles" in human life because they are so deeply anchored in Christian being. One of them is the missionary pastor of a faraway village; the other is a mother writing to her married daughter. They meet for the first time in these pages, but it seems they have drawn water from the same well.

V

More Things in Heaven and Earth

Dear Mrs. Adams:

Considering the tremendous social pressure put on Catholics to practice birth control, and in some countries government pressure; the economic, psychological, and physical problems of many families; and the number of Catholic couples who admittedly are practicing birth control, moral theologians are seeking desperately for an answer.

The moral theologian is especially concerned with the minimum: this much and no more can be demanded under pain of sin. His job is to eliminate as much sin as possible. Where there is doubt he wants to give the sinner as much freedom and benefit as possible. This approach very often emphasizes the negative, and the ideal is not even mentioned. It is dangerous because it can undermine spiritual ideals. But it is right insofar as it delineates our freedom—not to do the minimum, but to choose to do as much as God wills; and this, not necessarily under pain of sin or of damnation, but under pain of not becoming as perfect as God wants us to be. It is a question of vocation.

Marriage is a supernatural vocation. The Holy Father is especially concerned in safeguarding the supernatural character of marriage and all this involves. It is impossible to fulfill this from natural motives or by one's own strength. It demands the supernatural help of God. Therefore, even if scientists could perfect the rhythm method or if theologians could rationalize to a morally permissible use of the pill, the basic problem remains the acceptance of God's will in fulfilling one's vocation.

This may sound like begging the question, but I do not think it is. Even now the rhythm method cannot be used without a sufficient reason. Some theologians, concerned as they are with minimums, may say that any couple with four children have a morally sufficient reason. Such statements are dangerous because they have to be qualified. Perhaps every couple with four children can practice rhythm or some sort of family limitation without falling into mortal sin. But is that what God is asking from the majority of Catholic couples?

If they respond generously to what He asks of them, He will give the supernatural strength and everything else that is needed to fulfill their vocation. It involves such things as dedication to one's vocation, sacrifice, generosity, the value of the human soul, and love of God.

And this is just where many may object. It is fine to speak of sacrifice, generosity, love of God, etc. But what about unpaid bills, a drinking problem, children without clothes or proper medical care, someone teetering on the edge of mental breakdown? What about the very real and intense suffering, both physical and mental, that many Catholic couples are undergoing? Just how much do they have to take? Is there no relief? This is the critical question. The fact that a morally permissible means of escaping from their immediate suffering or an expected future suffering is available, does not mean that they should necessarily choose it as the best thing to do.

It *may* be the best way. But it is also conceivable that for some it is not the best way. The point is that the question should be decided not from the viewpoint of what will enable one to escape the burdens of his vocation, but from the viewpoint of what will enable one to bear his burdens and fulfill his vocation.

The question is not, "How do I escape?" but "How do I do God's will in the matter?" Or better, "Father, if it be possible, let this chalice pass from me. Yet not my will, but thine be done." Unless God's will is positively chosen, the result will be frustration and lesser perfection. It may even lead to permanent moral stagnation. At such a crisis in their life, a couple should be made aware of both their freedom to choose and the consequences of their choice.

We are free to a certain extent to determine our response to God's call and grace. And to a certain extent only the individual or couple concerned can determine how much God is asking and their response. Nor does God ask the same of any two individuals or any two couples. Sometimes, to our dismay, circumstances and events beyond our control may take away our choice and reveal God's will quite clearly.

In any case, of this we are sure: every supernatural vocation is demanding. God asks for everything unconditionally and takes as much as we give. To the extent that we give ourselves in supernatural love, to that extent do we become Godlike and fulfill our vocation.

Our approach and dispositions must be positive and supernatural: what is my vocation and its ideal fulfillment? Then, in accord with God's will insofar as I can know it, I must *strive* to fulfill my vocation. It is only in such a positive, supernatural approach that Catholic couples will find the peace and love that is properly theirs.

Any selfish attempt to escape the burdens of one's vocation necessarily leads to frustration. Selfishness is not an escape from suffering. It is the wound of suffering. Loving acceptance of God's will is its only cure. It is this selfishness which we all must seek to overcome, no matter what our vocation. Charity must be the guiding principle of any Christian vocation.

This is why I think "Love, O Love" is so important. The moral theologians' praiseworthy efforts and the birth control controversy are confusing people. The subtle reasoning, the public clash between theologians, the emphasis on the negative approach, the unclear and sometimes biased statements in the press, all add up to confusion and to a distortion of the truth. To some it must suddenly seem that Catholics have been wrong all along: that they should have been practicing birth control of some sort: that the couple with more than four children have sinned in irresponsibly having more children than was prudent, etc. Is the heroic suffering and generosity of many Catholic couples now being made to seem imprudent, foolish, and erroneous by those who guided them toward making such a complete supernatural response to their vocation?

"Love, O Love" points out the danger of negative thinking about marriage, and the danger of substituting some other insufficient guide for supernatural charity. And it recalls some basic truths which the Holy Spirit has taught us through the Holy Father and which, most of all in these times, we cannot afford to lose. If some subtle theological distinction or some new scientific fact or find gives us a morally permissible and scientifically sure method of family limitation, it will be even more necessary that your message be heard.   —Father M.

Dear Grace,

On our last visit we got into a discussion of "family planning"—remember? Everyone spoke out and lots of things were said, but ever since then I've wanted to write a few things just for you.

I remember very well how it was with Dad and me. We had the same problem you and all the other young married people have now. It's the biggest problem you'll have at this time. I had no one to consult, but I read everything I could, and I prayed and tried to find an answer. And I want to tell you, if I can, how to find your answer.

Grace, please don't feel that this letter is a sermon that I'm preaching, or that I feel in any way that my conclusions are the only possible conclusions. It's just that I love you so much I want to help you, even if I don't say anything you haven't already heard.

First, I feel that the only one who can help you is Our Lord. Ask Him what He wants you to do. We are all so different. He has placed us all here, He knows what He wants each of us to do. It may not be what *we* think at all. That's why we have to ask Him. Put yourself, your family, your life in His hands. *He* can't make a mistake in planning your life, but *you* can.

There were two times in my life that I was desperately fighting God's will, or what I thought was His will. Then when I stopped fighting and made up my mind to accept, I found out that the thing I was afraid of wasn't His will at all. But I couldn't find this out as long as I kept on fighting. Since then I can honestly say that whatever I feel God wants me to do, big or little, easy or difficult, that's what I try to do. This is what I was made for. I have learned to welcome what God sends and not to fight or worry, just to trust Him. Actually this is an *easy* way to live once you take it up.

To learn His will in my daily life I say a prayer to the Holy Ghost every morning. Then I go through the day confidently. There are always more jobs than I could possibly do, so I have to make a selection. I could never have raised eleven children, kept this big house, cooked, washed, ironed, and everything else by myself without spiritual help. So I had to know what the most necessary things were, one at a time.

I worked all day and rarely went anywhere. Even so the beds weren't always made, the rugs weren't always vacuumed, and the dust was often with me. But Daddy was so good. He never expected too much, he always understood how full my hands were.

Eventually I learned to try to live in God's presence. I have a cross I kiss many times during the day for help and guidance and because I want to love God more. I try to be at ease with my duties. I no longer go about my work using up all my strength worrying about what I still have to do. I go about each task as if it were the only one. When it's finished, I quietly ask the Lord about the next job.

On all big decisions I take care either to get to church to pray over them or I pray at home when I can be alone for a while. At first it was hard because I was expecting a direct answer right away. But I found that after I had spent time talking to God and to His Blessed Mother, I always got the grace not to *worry*, to leave it up to Him. That in itself is wonderful. Then, in His own way, God answers.

Now, as for your concern about rhythm and spacing your children, of course you and Tom must arrive at your own decision. But first ask God what *He* wants.

You say you are nervous and that you just can't have a large family. I think you should find out what makes you nervous. Don't just say you are nervous and do nothing about it. Suppose smoking makes you nervous (though I'm not saying it does!)? Well, then, try to cut down. Ask God's help. It would be better to give up smoking *if* necessary than to give up having children.

Everyone has some excuse for not having children. Some people do have real problems, I know, but why must giving up babies always be the solution? Of course, poor health, lack of money, etc., all *can* be reasons. If they are, then more than ever one needs God's help—much more, I think, than in any trials that come with raising a large family.

You and I chose marriage. God's intention for marriage is to bring His children into the world. He didn't make marriage for two people to have two cars, expensive furniture, boats and all the things I see so many spending their whole lives achieving. (By the way have you noticed that the modern equipment and appliances which are supposed to make life so simple actually seem to make it so hard . . . . why is that?)

I don't know anyone my age who has enjoyed life more or who is in better health than I am now. Not being able to have children or perhaps being able to have only two or three could be a much bigger problem than anything connected with a large family, it seems to me. Even if someone does find a way of family limitation that the Church approves of, I still feel that having children is the *easier* way to live the married state and the happiest and most rewarding way.

I divide a woman's life into 20-year periods. The first 20 years are easy and carefree. The next 20 are working years, and the last 20 are the rewarding ones. Why try to see how small we can make our reward? Why not work for the biggest reward possible?

Grace, I know it may be hard for you to accept this now. But be patient with yourself. When you are young you like to do lots of things that in a few years will not interest you. God knows this. Put your trust in Him. Go from day to day, from hour to hour even.

These years are the hardest, I think, but once Jimmy can do a few things for himself you will find it all begin to get easier. At fifty-two I still have seven children at home, but they all take care of themselves pretty much. I would be just as confined if there were only Mark left, and I wouldn't be nearly as happy. Jane, Marian, Dan, Peter, Terry, and Cathy are a joy and bring me so much love.

With each child your heart grows bigger with love; you acquire patience too as you grow older. Then, after being married thirty years as I am, with a husband you love more than ever, you'll feel at times you will just burst with happiness.

If you and Tom are praying and feel you have sufficient reason for using rhythm or for abstaining for a few months after birth, you can without fear of doing wrong. But first, ask what God wants. Make your decisions together with Him. If we only could sense how much He loves us when we try to please Him. Whether you have two or ten children is something for God to decide. I promise you will be completely happy at my age if you have put your faith in God and His Blessed Mother and accepted what He plans.

I have written so much. I wish I could have said it in just a few lines. You are a loving child and so kind. You have always made Daddy and me very happy. And we love Tom and your two beautiful babies. The two of you have made a wonderful start in your family life. I am praying that you will learn to let God work the rest out for you.

With all my love,

Mother

Part Two

..Other articles were appearing too, giving valuable insights into some of the problems for which the standard, unimaginative, and ultimately dehumanizing solution is always less babies.

Some of the following deal with medical, economic, and social questions, two concentrate on philosophical and theological considerations. And one is here, like the court jester, to remind us that human wisdom can be pitifully funny.

I

As Christ Loved The Church

Thomas Burke

Father Burke is a priest of the Middlesbrough Diocese, England. He is the author of a book on Christian marriage entitled The Gold Ring. *The following article appeared in* The Way Magazine, *a London publication.*

The beginning of the book of Genesis has about it a deceptive simplicity. The story of the creation of the universe is sung in a litany of transparent phrases, 'God said, Let light begin . . .

Let a solid vault rise amid the waters . . . Let dry land appear', and so on, each with its doxology. 'And God saw that it was good'.[1] But before man is called to the scene, there is a pause, a deliberation as it were: 'Then God said, Let us make man to our own image and likeness'. And to the simple statement, 'God created man in his own image', is added something more complex and mysterious, 'Male and female he created them'.[2] It would seem that the inspired author wished to imply that in this twofold creation, in all that is man and woman, in the power to love and to perfect love in creation, there is a profound image of the God who is love and whose love is perfected in his creation.

If men of today are conditioned to view sex with shame and confusion, Adam, in the garden of delight, saw in it the splendor of a divine masterpiece and greeted it with an enthusiasm which the holy writer's words seem to echo: 'And God brought her to the man and he cried out, This at last is bone of my bones and flesh of my flesh'.[3] He saw not only an image of himself, but also of God, in whose image male and female are created.

THE IMAGE OF SEX DEFACED

It is certain that one of the consequences of the first sin was to deface the image of sex. Adam's enthusiasm was changed to accusation: 'She it was who gave me the fruit and I did eat', and the innocence of sex perished, 'I was naked and ashamed'. It would be interesting to trace the history of the image. Primitive peoples, though recognizing it as something holy, were

1. *Gen.* 1, 1-25.
2. *Gen.* 1, 26-27.
3. *Gen.* 2, 22-23.

ignorant of its meaning. They attributed to their deities not only love and creation, but also human bodies, making of them male and female gods who united and copulated with grossness, and betraying all the passions of human frailty. There appears to be little difference between these ancient idolatries and that modern confusion which is unable to read the image at all, for the pagan of today sees in sex no more than an instinct which man shares with the animals; the only difference is that he is intelligent enough to vitiate its purpose when it suits him.

GOD'S MARRIAGE TO THE HUMAN RACE

The inspired teaching of the prophets progressively revealed to man that the mystery which he possessed, the instinct which caused him to leave father and mother and to cleave to a woman in fidelity, is a privileged participation in the holiness and fidelity of God, a true image of God's own love: his special love for his chosen people.

In speaking of God's marriage to the human race, we must regard the Old Testament more properly as a time of courtship. It remained for the Incarnation to bring about the consummation: for it is in the Incarnation, in the person of Jesus Christ, that God and man are united, two in one flesh. 'Today', we sing in a Christmastide antiphon, 'the Church is united to her heavenly Spouse and the Magi have brought their gifts to the Royal Nuptials'.

This parallel between God's union with humanity and the human device of matrimony is no coincidence nor accident, but rather a part of God's eternal plan. Just as there is one essential man, Jesus Christ, of whom Adam was the prototype and all other men are a variety of copies, so too there is one essential marriage, that of Christ and his Church, and in the divine plan all other marriages are envisaged as copies of it. It was such knowledge of the Old Testament tradition, coupled with the teaching of our Lord, that led St. Paul to say to the Ephesians: Husbands, love your wives as Christ loved the Church'.[4] In the theology of St. Paul, Christian marriage has this vocation and this dignity: it is to be modeled on the union of Christ and the Church.

THE INVOLVEMENT OF MATRIMONY

Every Christian, by his baptism, is both re-created according to the image and likeness of Christ, and is incorporated into his mystical body, hence it follows that the likeness of Christ and of His Church is represented in both partners of a Christian marriage. But matrimony, like every sacrament, constitutes its own particular involvement with Christ. It is the sacrament which commits those who receive it to the Christ who loves the Church. No matter how unconscious they may be of it or how unaware of their dignity, when Christians marry, a union is completed which is a model of the great union, the great marriage, between Christ and his Church, and a twofold demand is laid on husband and wife. First of all each must learn to recognise and then to honor in the other partner an image of Christ and the Church, and secondly each must strive to conform his own person to that image, and together with the partner perfect the image of that union.

THE HUSBAND 'AS CHRIST'

Let us first speak of the role of the husband, who is to make

4. Eph. 5, 25.

42

himself 'as Christ' to his wife. There are, of course, many ways of being 'as Christ': the hermit, the missionary, the martyr all imitate Christ, but the man who is married must be to his wife 'as Christ to the Church'. That is, he must be her head as king and prophet, and he must give himself up for her as priest and victim.

Christ is the king of the Church, first of all, because he created it and brought it into being. St. Augustine, drawing a parallel from Eve born from the side of Adam, says the Church was born from the side of Christ hanging on the cross. The husband following his vocation to imitate Christ, presents a third parallel, for he too 'creates' his wife, his family and his home.

The kingdom of marriage is more than a union of two people; it is a home and a family. Here too, the husband is the king-creator. It is the natural instinct of every young man who thinks of marriage to attempt to possess a home of his own, which will be the context of his life and love. It is as natural as the bird carrying a twig for the nest; but for the Christian husband it is a true imitation of Christ. It is the foundation of a church, since the Christian family is the fundamental unit of the Church, and itself a church in miniature. Thus a task as prosaic as visiting a building society or papering a room or fitting a cupboard, because of its purpose, shares in the dignity of building a cathedral or a shrine.

HIS FRUITFULNESS

The family, it is true, comes into being from the body of the mother; but the parallel still holds. She gives her children life, her blood nourishes them and she gives them birth; but her ability to do all this depends on the power given to her by her hus-

43

band. Without him she is capable of nothing; for it is he who enlivens her body and makes it fruitful. The Easter vigil liturgy forcibly draws the simile of Christ's work in the Church's womb, the baptismal font. With an unmistakable clarity of symbolism the Christ-candle is plunged into the font: 'May the power of the Holy Spirit come down into this filled font, and may it fertilize all the substance of this water with the power of effecting new birth'.

HIS PRIESTHOOD

Those ancient civilizations which recognized the patriarchs as leaders and teachers of their communities often gave them another role: that of priest. In this they followed a natural instinct; for if the father is to represent the family before men, he is also to represent it before God, to offer its prayers and sacrifices and to seek God's blessings on it. By the sacrament of baptism every Christian is incorporated into Christ and therefore is a sharer in Christ's priesthood, but it is the office of the head of the family to intercede for his family, to seek God's blessings on it and to offer sacrifice for it. There is something touching about a mother assisting her children to lisp their night prayers, but family prayer led by the father of the household has an unsurpassing dignity.

A priest is more than a prayer-leader: he is called upon to offer sacrifice. The priest-head of the family, in his imitation of Christ, is to prove himself a Christ-like priest and victim, offering himself for his church. A man's offering is first of all of himself; and marriage means a constant subordination of the claims of self to the claims of the family. Anyone who marries 'for himself', from any egoistic or sensuous motive, finds only disap-

44

pointment and frustration; rather he must constantly sacrifice his self-will, self-expression and self-exaltation for the sake of the whole family. For the majority of men there is another form of sacrifice; the long hours and hard physical labor necessary to provide a home, security and education for the family. There are some men who undertake such a labor from ambition; and these are occasionally disappointed when their children fail them. Others labor for generous motives of love; but for the truly Christian man this labor is an act of heroic virtue. He sees in it an imitation of the Good Shepherd, giving up his life for his sheep.

THE WIFE 'AS THE CHURCH'

If the husband is the Christ of a marriage, his wife is called on to be an imitation of the Church. It is now time to consider what this involves and how she must characterize the Church in its relationship to Christ.

Much of what is involved for the wife follows logically from what we have said about the role of the husband. If he is the leader she is the led; he the teacher, she the taught. All this is summarized in one word, 'docility', which may be defined as 'being easy to teach and willing to obey'.

HER DOCILITY

There are some who regard the marriage promise to obey as an anachronism; but such people have a tendency to regard any obedience whatsoever as an anachronism and incompatible with human dignity. Equality, of course, exists between man and woman, the equality of human dignity and personality before God; but that equality in no way destroys the reality of the difference with which God has endowed woman nor the superiorities with which he has enhanced her, superiorities of beauty, graciousness, intuition and patience, to name but a few. Her body, her intellect and her emotions all speak of a difference, a difference of purpose which does not outrival the male accomplishments but completes them.

If her role of obedience springs from the very nature of her being, then its accomplishment finds its source in love. Just as all men's obedience to God is a work of love, for not only are we commanded to love but, by love, we freely obey; so too the wife's obedience has a two-fold source in love: in the love for the person of her husband and in the love for what he represents.

HER FRUITFULNESS

The Church is not only the obedient spouse of Christ; she also glories in her fruitfulness. She gives him his children from generation to generation, until the number of the elect will be complete. She is the mother of those children who are born in the womb of her font, and whose education Christ entrusts to her. In this also a wife is called to be an imitation and a representation of the Church. It would seem that we are now moving into the era of the planned family, a time when parents will be able to choose freely for themselves the number of their children and at the same time will be able to use their marriage with little more restriction than that imposed by Friday abstinence or the Sunday Mass obligation. It will be a blessing if such knowledge removes from marital relations the desire to have recourse to sinful means; there is however the danger that the fruitfulness intended by God will be deliberately avoided for selfish or hedonistic motives. The reasons which permit husband and wife to limit their fruitfulness are summarized by Pope Pius XII in his celebrated allocution to midwives under four heads—eugenic, economic, medical and social. The problem for the future will be in the application of these criteria to individual cases: an honest solution to it will be possible only for those families who have a fundamental desire for supernaturally motivated fruitfulness and see the excusing causes as impediments to their aspirations rather than excuses from fulfilling their obligations. Such a desire for fruitfulness will run against the current of public opinion. It will frequently mean mockery and derision, it will often cause suffering and labor; but it also brings its rewards both in this world and on that day when generation after generation will proclaim their parents and enter with them into the Kingdom.

THEIR LOVE

Having spoken of the role of husband and of wife in their imitation of Christ and of the Church there remains a word to be said on their mutual love: that too must be a replica of the love which unites Christ and the Church. As we have already seen, Christian marriage transforms the poles from and to which the current of love flows, since each husband is called on to be Christ and love as Christ and each wife to be the Church and love as the Church; therefore love itself takes on a supernatural character and becomes, in all reality, charity.

Like Christ's own charity, marital love must be sacrificial. The husband, as priest-victim, must consume his life for his family; the wife and mother, in her obedience and in the burdens involved in her fruitfulness, is also committed to a life of sacrifice. For either of them, such a life can be no more than a burden unless it is inspired by a charity which gives meaning to sacrifice, and seeks in the work of sacrifice a religious act offered to God and intended to bring his blessings on the family.

Finally, Christ loves the Church with an eternal love; so too the love of marriage must have about it the quality of eternity and endurance. It goes without saying that it is destined to endure throughout the life-time of the partners; but St. Paul, in his advice to widows[5] and the Church, in her refusal to repeat the nuptial blessing, would seem to stretch it into eternity. Hence if we began this consideration by seeing marriage as a replica of God's love brought out of Eden, we can also see it as a foretaste of the supreme love which every man is destined to enjoy in the great marriage of Christ and the Church, to be consummated in the eternal court of heaven.

5. *I Cor.* 7, 40.

II

Children

L. MICHAEL CURTIN

Father Curtin, a priest of Opus Dei, is chaplain of Northview Cultural Center on the north side of Chicago. A graduate physicist from Harvard, he has a doctorate in theology from the Lateran University. Children *is condensed from a talk.*

"Let us make man to our image and likeness . . ."[1] God communicated His perfections to His creature and made him the image of His glory. Divinely prolific in His trinitarian intimacy, He gave man the power of reproduction so that many men could share His glory.

Even after the fall and the beginning of death, the human species was to perpetuate itself on earth. The growth of the human race was still to multiply those who, through salvation, would be the family of God.

Even without sin or death, explains St. Thomas, "in the state of innocence there would have been generation to multiply the number of men . . ."[2] In animals (and, in general, among living beings which do not have a spiritual soul) the aim of generation is the conservation of the species, for the individuals are not

1. *Gen.* 1,26.
2. *S.Th.* I, q.98, a. 1 c.

perpetual but die and disappear. In man, who besides having a corruptible body has an immortal soul, nature's principal aim in generation is both the conservation of the species and the multiplication of the individuals who will remain forever.

WHY MULTIPLY?

The human creature has "a special reason to multiply himself and that is to complete the number of the elect."[3] And since this number is very large ("a great multitude which no man could number"),[4] those called to matrimony are called to co-operate generously with the Creator.

Our Lord sent His apostles out on all the roads of the earth, free from human ties, to invite all to the house of the Father. For the same end He instituted the sacrament of matrimony on the basis of a natural reality. Sacramental grace makes husband and wife unite in a holy way to bring children into the world and to work actively to make them children of God. The Mystical Body of Christ, which has to reach its complete development, the "perfect age,"[5] depends on this sacrament. "Through Holy Orders the Church is governed and spiritually propagated. Through matrimony, on the other hand, She is increased in body."[6] The primary end of matrimony is children: their generation and their Christian education. What a wonderful participation of parents in the general mission of the Church!

SACRIFICE AND JOY

To collaborate in the task of completing the number of the

3. *S.Th.* I, q.72, a. 1 ad 4.
4. *Apoc.* VIII, 9.
5. *Eph.* IV, 13
6. Conc. of Florence, *decr. pro Armenis.*

50

elect would have been easy for man if he had not violated the order established by God. But since original sin, any human task entails sacrifices. This is true of the work of procreation, bringing new human beings to Christian maturity.

The Blessed Virgin was no stranger to the sufferings that sometimes pierce the souls of parents. The poverty of Bethlehem—she had so few things to offer to her Son and her God. The persecution of Herod and the arduous flight into Egypt. The loss of Jesus in Jerusalem: "Behold, thy father and I have been seeking thee sorrowing."[7] The natural austerity of Nazareth in the home of an artisan. The departure of Jesus to fulfill his ministry among the people. The inconceivable agony of Golgatha.

Sacrifices exist. Love itself demands them. But sacrifice is not necessarily sorrow. In the majority of cases, sorrows cannot dim the joy that children bring, a joy that is multiplied in Christian families because, through Baptism, children become members of the Mystical Body.

Joy and sorrow, blessings and sacrifices, gladness and suffering! God, in instituting matrimony with children as the primary and supreme end, gave it a form consisting "of a certain indivisible union of spirits, which each one of the parties would bind himself to preserve undivided."[8] In this love which unites them and which constitutes the soul of matrimony, spouses find solid help in overcoming obstacles and difficulties. This is even more true in Christian marriage where conjugal affection is a love in Christ, supernaturalized, not only as all Christian love, but also in the proximate and specific finality of

7. *Luke* II, 48.
8. *S.Th.* III, q.29, a. 2 c.

marital love: giving children to God.

Sacrifices exist. Love itself demands them. For that reason, parents must instill in themselves "an unshakable confidence in Divine Providence and a determination to accept the inescapable sacrifices and hardships involved in so noble and important a task as the co-operation with God in the transmitting of human life and the bringing up of children."[9]

When this order of things is not taken into account, it is logical not to want to have children, even to the point of considering them a nuisance to be avoided—forgetting that the secondary ends of matrimony are licit and meritorious only when the primary end is respected.

THE HUNGRY*

Because concupiscence and the inclination to avoid effort are strong, man can always find apparent reasons for eluding the ordination of God. There is, for example, the world-wide movement which, under the guise of justice and philanthropy, proposes the massive diminution and control of births as a remedy to free mankind from hunger and misery.

Part of mankind today does not have sufficient food; in some places the problem is especially acute. But half the world remains unpopulated; there is an indefinite number of still untapped resources; and there are countries where the problem is excessive production of goods. To alleviate economic misery, generous cooperation should be sought among nations. Produc-

9. John XXIII, enc. *Mater et Magistra.*

*No attempt at a full treatment of this very complicated subject can be made here. Further points are made in *The Economics of Population* by Colin Clark, which follows, and in the excerpts from *Mater et Magistra* in Part Three.

tion should be stimulated in underdeveloped countries. Those who enjoy abundance should feel the urgent need to help those in need, instead of unburdening their consciences by offering them antinatural and unmerciful "solutions."

There is something spurious in these persistent efforts to impede the birth of new men. It often happens that the countries where these practices are widespread are countries with a flourishing economy. In due time, however, the sad results of their philosophy become evident in their entire social structure.

RATIONAL CONTROL?

Another argument put forward in favor of "family planning" is the use of human reason—submitting the natural reproductive function to the dominion of one's will; making this act more human, more rational and free, by having the children one wants, if one wants and when one wants; making the marital act "more moral" with a "programming" of the children according to the circumstances of the family.

This argument mixes up several points. First, simple rationalizing on human behavior does not make it good or bad, for reasoning itself is not the measure of the morality of acts. "The fact that human reason is the norm of human will and that by which is measured the degree of its goodness, is derived from the eternal law, which is identified with divine reason itself. . . . Consequently, it is clear that the goodness of the human will depends much more on the eternal law than on human reason."[10]

Therefore before knowing how to do things, man ought to know what things he ought to do and why, and what things he ought not to do and also why. In general it is evident that since

10. S.Th. I-II ae, q. 19, a. 4.

the end of matrimony is children, married people should want to have them. He who does not want to have children (assuming there is some positive reason for this) should not get married.

What if two people want to have children, but only so many and no more? This is as improper as wanting so many years of marriage and no more. Even if today there is a more exact knowledge of the fertile cycles and it is possible to construct fairly accurate charts, matrimonial ethics are not dependent on technical solutions. It would be immoral to reduce the marital act to a simple means of pleasure.

In some concrete cases, taking advantage of the advice of the priest and of the doctor, if there are serious reasons for not wanting children and at the same time moral or physical difficulties involved in avoiding the generative act, periodic continence may be allowed. What has to be asked is if God wants this new child. We have to serve the will of God and not limit ourselves to simple biological criteria. We must also avoid assuming that the agreement of the spouses is sufficient to produce a new life. Life "from its inception requires the direct action of God, the Creator."[11]

Rational control, besides violating the primary end of matrimony and producing social evils (which even many neo-malthusians are today beginning to realize) morally degrades those who practice it without grave reasons. It can produce biological and psychological disturbances since it limits the use of matrimony to the naturally least appropriate periods.

"Genesis reminds us that God gave two commandments to our first parents (Gen. 1,28): that of transmitting life: 'be fruitful and multiply'; and that of subduing nature: 'fill the earth and

11. John XXIII, enc. *Mater et Magistra.*

subdue it.' These commandments complement one another. Certainly the divine command to subdue nature was not given for destructive ends. It rather assigns them to the service of human life."[12]

In order for a marriage to be what God wants, it is not enough not to pervert its nature. It is necessary besides to use the means to fulfill its end. If the husband and wife acquire some rights by marrying, they also contract certain obligations. "To embrace marriage, to continually use the faculty proper to it and lawful in it alone, and, on the other hand, to withdraw always and deliberately with no serious reason from its primary obligation, would be a sin against the very meaning of conjugal life."[13] One cannot then, flatly state that it is licit to use the marriage act exclusively on those days on which nature has deprived the woman of the capacity to conceive. This cannot even be stated when no attack is made on the nature of the act itself, even when one is ready to accept and educate the child that might be born from a possible "error."

"You and I," Msgr. Escrivá de Balaguer has said, "would not love God nor serve Him, if our parents had practiced this theory. I put to shame the married couples who do not want to have children. If you do not want to have children, practice continence! I think and I sincerely say that it is not Christian to recommend abstinence in those periods when nature has given the woman the capacity to conceive. In some particular, very concrete cases, always taking advantage of the advice of the doctor and priest, it could and ought to be permitted. But never can it be recommended as a general rule." The circumstances

12. *Ibid.*
13. Pius XII, address, 10/29/51.

that could lead a married couple to practice periodic continence will always have to be proportionately grave, independently of the will of the parties. The pros and cons and the reasons which exclude the advisability of perfect continence will have to be properly evaluated.

THE RESPONSIBILITY FOR EDUCATION

In order to justify "family planning" a point is raised about the responsibility for educating the children, the financial possibilities of the family, and even the possibilities of personal attention in training them well. This argument is a temporization. "God also visits large families with His Providence, and parents, especially those who are poor, give clear testimony to this by resting all their trust in Him when human efforts are not enough. A trust that has a solid foundation and is not in vain! Providence—to put it in human words and ideas—is not the sum total of exceptional acts of divine pity; it is the ordinary result of harmonious activity on the part of the infinite wisdom, goodness and omnipotence of the Creator. God will never refuse a means of living to those He calls into being."[14]

God is the Creator, intervening directly in each new life, and He is provident. To accept the children He wants to send is not to "tempt" Him. To tempt Him is to seek ways to frustrate the end of matrimony, at the same time enjoying its physical pleasures. We seek His kingdom and His justice when we desire to give Him children who will love and serve Him, when we want to use matrimony for His purposes.

Besides, we must keep in mind that Christian education is

14. Pius XII, address 1/20/58.

fundamentally a question of training in virtue which makes the way to heaven easier. And where could this education be given better than in a home faithful to the divine prescriptions, where the parents love and respect one another and gladly sacrifice themselves in order to give God children? What better school of virtue and generosity?

THE CHRISTIAN FAMILY

In the face of widespread fear of new life, it is necessary to spread Christian truth so that the consciences of married people are enlivened with the exact knowledge of the greatness of their mission and of all their obligations, and so that a virtuous disposition of generosity will be fostered in their souls.

"You can give irrefutable proofs of the stupidity of birth-control theories and of the harm that comes from putting them into practice. As long as there is no sincere determination to let the Creator carry on His work as He chooses, then human selfishness will always find new sophistries and excuses to still the voice of conscience (to the extent it can), and to carry on abuses. The value of the testimony offered by the parents of large families lies not only in their unequivocal and forceful rejection of any deliberate compromise between the law of God and human selfishness, but also in their readiness to accept joyfully and gratefully these priceless gifts of God—their children—in whatever number it may please Him to send them. This kind of attitude frees married couples from oppressive anxieties and remorse, and in the opinion of outstanding doctors, creates the ideal psychological conditions for the healthy development of children born of the marriage. Right at the beginning of these new lives it eliminates all those worries and disturbances that can so easily leave physical or psychological scars on the mother or child.

"Wherever you find large families in great numbers, they point to the physical and moral health of a Christian people, a living faith in God and trust in His Providence, and fruitful and joyful holiness of Christian marriage."[15]

Good spreads itself. When one lives rightly and so reaches the true value of life, he wants to make others participate in this good. "What we love for itself, we want to be the best and, in so far as possible, that it be perfected and multiplied."[16] When there is true love between a married couple and not merely carnal desire, it is natural, and supernatural, for them to want to perpetuate themselves in their children, in spite of the sacrifices that this may bring.

This is especially true in a Christian family sanctified by the sacrament, where the children are called to be other Christs. In a truly Christian family the children are received as a blessing from God, as a crown, as a proof of predilection and of confidence. God puts into the hands of parents those incipient lives called to participate in the divine nature through grace and to form the joyous court of God in heaven. And when this proof of confidence is repeatedly renewed, as in large families, it has to be received gratefully as a very special blessing and as a particular promise of assistance.

The virtues of a home can be better lived in such families, because there are greater reasons for dedication, for the giving of oneself, and fewer occasions for selfishness. The reasons for joy and happiness are multiplied. Sorrows are mitigated,

15. *Ibid.*
16. *Summa contra Gentiles,* 1,75.

are more easily borne, because they are shared in a unity of spirit.

When there are many children, there are some for every walk of life. Some can give themselves completely to God, dedicating themselves to serve Him and to serve souls in an apostolic celibacy. Others can serve God in marriage, and continue the family. "I have seen many married couples," writes Msgr. Escrivá de Balaguer, "who, even when Our Lord does not give them more than one child, still have the generosity to give that child to God. But there are not too many who do so. In large families it is easier to understand the greatness of a divine vocation, and among their children there are some for every state in life. But I have also experienced, with thanks to God—and not just a few times—that others, to whom Our Lord does not give a family even though their married lives are exemplary, accept with joy the holy will of God and dedicate more time to charity toward their neighbors. I pray to Our Lord that there be large families. Why should we keep so many possible creatures from blessing, praising and loving God? This propaganda on birth control, that can never be sufficiently abhorred, is diabolical."

Moreover, children, the family, for married members of Opus Dei, has become a way to sanctity that the Church has specifically recognized and blessed—a divine vocation which leads them to accept the children God sees fit to send them. They find a thousand things that lead them to God in the efforts they have to make in order to support and educate those children. And if God generously rewarded that servant who returned the talents with interest, how will He reward those who with sacrifice and dedication return to Him these fruits of eternal life, their children, who are, each one of them, Christ Himself!

III

How Many Children?

J. URTEAGA

Father Urteaga, S.T.D., is vice-rector of the Basilica of St. Michael in Madrid, and editor of Mundo Cristiano. *His books include* Man the Saint *and* God and Children. *This article appeared in* Mundo Cristiano *for May, 1963.*

Would you like a mathematical formula for finding out how many children to have? I'm sorry, but I can't give you one. Nobody can.

Recently I suggested a simple formula for deciding how much alms to give. Some people thought it was excessively generous. Others thought it was miserly.

The number of children for a Christian family has some relation to the formula for almsgiving. It is God who, in the last instance, is asking for children and material help. Children for heaven and money for the poor. And the only useful formula is that of generosity.

Are you disappointed? Well, no other formula has ever been found. I don't want to scare anyone, though. Do you have problems of housing, money, health? You cannot have more children? Well, don't lose your peace. God is with you.

But please let me sing of generosity. And please don't worry about sinning through liberality. One can perhaps err by bringing too many children into a shack, as one can perhaps err by giving excessive alms without regard for the material needs of the family. But has anyone ever committed a sin of excessive almsgiving? This is one sin I haven't yet heard confessed.

Do you really think there is danger ahead because our families have too many children? Nonsense. If you want to protest something, protest the crimes being committed in Japan—two million assassinations, two million abortions! But please don't criticize those who sacrifice themselves to give more children to God. Surely you don't imagine some people have children the way others collect stamps?

Last week I received an ad for another one of those books in which couples are taught how to regulate offspring—without sinning, of course. The book claims to offer a new method—simple, natural, and effective. I don't believe it. And I don't like the phrase, "Married people, doctors, and priests can profit from reading this book." Believe me, you can derive many things from reading such a book, but no fruit whatsoever. Books like this are full of tables. Not, however, the addition or multiplication tables—only division, reduction.

Generous parents of large families: you must face an unjust world which does not understand you. Expect your sacrifice to be called excessive and your faithfulness to be called madness. Take refuge in God who loves us to excess and is asking us for faithful love without limit.

Do you remember the words of Judas in the Gospel? He begins by calling Mary, the sister of Lazarus, extravagant because she used a jar of expensive ointment for the feet of Jesus. He ends by preaching a sermon—the only sermon we keep of the traitor—a sermon with very few words: "I have betrayed innocent blood."

Generous parents, listen to God's loving words to you, spoken by Pope John: "We especially enjoy entering those homes where there lives a numerous family, a living witness of faithfulness to God, a concrete proof of abandonment to God's providence."

IV

French Awakening

GARY MAC EOIN

Gary Mac Eoin writes for many diocesan newspapers. This excerpt was published in The Pittsburgh Catholic.

The French people have gradually come to understand the falsity of the philosophy of Planned Parenthood, or as the French call it, neo-Malthusianism. Perhaps where they first saw it break down was in the economic sphere. The effort to freeze a given level of material wealth and comfort, to insure a little more for each by reducing the number of sharers, brought about the deterioration of France and its steady lag behind its competitors, whose rising populations insured an internal dynamism to spur economic progress.

More fundamentally, however, they have gradually come to grips with the more intimate problem. Whatever the protestations or the intentions of its proponents, the universal effect of the introduction of a neo-Malthusian mentality into a given society has been the perversion of the role of sex in the life of the married couple. It has encouraged a popularized Freudianism which presented self-control as a danger to physical and mental health and reduced the husband-wife relationship to a purely biological function. In addition, it played a big part in

63

the fixation on the physical aspects of sex which characterizes much of today's popular literature, theatre and movies, and which the Communists exploit gleefully as evidence of the decadence of bourgeois capitalism.

What the French have discovered is that for the individual husband and wife, the fruits of this philosophy are bitter. It is not simply that childless old age can be joyless, for that does not automatically follow. It is that the internal unity of the marriage itself is shattered by the very terms in which its expression is defined as the selfish satisfaction by two individuals of their individual and uncontrollable instincts. Instead of a growing together, there is a growing apart; instead of love, there is apathy, indifference, distaste, frigidity and hatred.

For the wife, in particular, what began as a liberation is soon an enslavement to the whims of her husband, a legalized prostitution which humiliates and lowers her. Because of the uncertainty of techniques, the relationship is always tinged by fear. The accidental child is unwanted. And remember that all of this is on the purely natural level, without taking into account the moral tortures of the many who feel they are cheating the purpose for which they pronounced their marriage vows.

V

The Rock Book

Herbert Ratner, M.D., is Director of Public Health, Oak Park, Illinois, and associate clinical professor of preventive medicine and public health at the Stritch School of Medicine, Loyola University, Chicago. He is a well-known lecturer on medicine and family life. "Medicine", his interview with Donald McDonald is one of a series on American Character published by the Center for the Study of Democratic Institutions. This article appeared in The Commonweal, *July 5, 1963.*

Dr. John Rock's *The Time Has Come* presents itself as "a Catholic doctor's proposals to end the battle over birth control" through a "sensitive probing of current theology." These proposals are most satisfactory when they embody or support solid Catholic thinking; for example, Father John Courtney Murray's position that the Connecticut statute against contraception is indefensible; and Family Life Bureau Director Msgr. John Knott's endorsement of an expanded governmental research program of reproductive physiology. They are insensitive and less than satisfactory when Dr. Rock is on his own or bolsters his positions with opinion that hardly can be considered cogent; for example, the elucidation of his belief that the contraceptive use of oral steroids (the Pill) is morally right; or his exposition and application of natural law.

Most of his less than satisfactory proposals stem from a chronic ambiguity which is characteristic of the book. We see this clearly in Chapter 11, *Straws in the Winds,* and Chapter 12, *A Proper Public Policy on Birth Control.* Here, in discussing birth control policy in public hospitals and public welfare programs, he keeps interchanging *family planning* and *medically indicated birth control.* He leads the reader to believe that the decision to approve the latter is the same as the approval of the former. His conclusion, however, does not follow from the preceding discussion.

Although there is plenty of room for disagreement in the United States as to what constitutes a medical indication, the fact remains that in a liberal profession like medicine there is a firm distinction between a physician prescribing birth control (or sterilization and abortion) to his diseased patient for therapeutic and preventive reasons and the state using a physician as an instrument to assuage political, social and economic metaphorical sicknesses by decimating indigent people as if they were diseases. On the part of welfare programs the overt motivation, in many instances, is the reduction of tax expenditures, the covert motivation is the protection of the state against human liabilities. This is not a religious issue, though men of religion may be interested in it. Rather it is a question of whether it is salutary for the medical profession to permit its members to become obeisant government technicians in this highly personal area of human privilege or whether family planning should be kept out of the hands of government by keeping it in the hands of voluntary agencies and thereby insulating the indigent against political pressure.

Furthermore, and I add this at the risk of being misunderstood, we should question whether it is good for the profession to become rich servants of the public by serving their wants and desires dissociated from their needs. In other areas of contemporary medical practice, capitulation to unenlightened patients' personal desires is leading to the ruin of medicine. We see this in the misuse of tranquilizers, stimulants, sedatives and antibiotics through consumer pressure. One of the stark facts of U.S. history is that contraception, which was introduced and promoted primarily for the lower classes because of their economic problems, was not used by them but was used instead with avidity by the middle and upper classes who did not have this problem as we normally recognize it. It is not known that in one of the richest areas of life, family life, this has made them happier. Obviously complex issues and complex solutions are involved. There is no indication, however, that Dr. Rock is aware of them. With the assistance of the science of demography he makes the population problem simply a numbers game.

The fact remains, however, that we have a genuine underpopulation of the middle and upper classes. The indigent of this country and the world—and they are indigent by virtue of exploitation and the indifference of whose who are better off—cannot pull themselves up by their own bootstraps. They desperately need teachers, physicians, social workers, engineers and the help of other professional and technical disciplines, to say nothing of moral leaders. We need them for the Peace Corps, both foreign and domestic, for assistance programs, for missionary enterprises of all kinds. Ironically, we would even need them to implement birth control programs, were that the solution to their problems. In the fight for the preservation of the traditions of western democracy we presumably need them for the cold war if we are to save Africa, Asia and Latin America.

Our greatest export need today is people. Only minds can save minds. During this interim adjustment period in world history, the world leans heavily on the middle and upper classes of this country whose children alone, at present, can take advantage of the rich opportunity offered them educationally. By ignoring these and other factors, Dr. Rock's analysis is superficial and underlies his ambiguities.

These ambiguities seem to stem from Dr. Rock's current need to wed Catholic doctrine to his own highly personalized views by stretching and accommodating the Church's teaching to his own lifelong professional beliefs and practices. Through this wedding he hopes to make a contribution in the area of Catholic and non-Catholic conflict. Unfortunately, his book, in my opinion, rather than contributing to a useful dialogue between Catholics and non-Catholics, or even among Catholics, obstructs dialogue. In this regard it is radically different from *Birth Control and Public Policy,* Catholic lawyer Norman St. John-Stevas' study issued by the Center for the Study of Democratic Institutions. The difference centers about the question—and it is most pertinent—of whether Dr. Rock's book truly represents a Catholic doctor's proposals. It is precisely Dr. Rock's personal and public insistence that he is talking as a "dedicated Roman Catholic" that confounds the dialogue. Without questioning the subjective truth of his conviction or his personal piety, what is essential for fruitful discussion is to differentiate Dr. Rock's "own religious and physiologic insights" which he puts forth to advance "everything that has given meaning to (his) life" from the universal position of his Church. The book itself confuses these positions and thus invokes dissonance and contradiction in its varied readers.

We witness that non-Catholic physicians and laymen hasten to praise his Catholic theology, extol the Doctor's Catholic devoutness, and in varying degrees clout his church. On the other hand Catholic theologians despair over his theology, reserve to the Doctor the privacy of his spiritual life, and over-respect his science. Some Catholics experience wish-fulfillment and compassionate attraction. Other Catholics ask, "What the hell is going on?" It is to the last question—this widespread misunderstanding —that I principally address myself. My general direction comes from the distinction in using *Catholic* as an adjective or a noun: the distinction between "a Catholic doctor or painter" and "a doctor or painter who is a Catholic."

Dr. Rock is a research physician most noted in scientific circles for his work on early human embryos. This work, which dates back to 1938, is referred to in his book. His embryos were recovered from *pregnant* women undergoing *elective* hysterectomies. Other embryos were obtained in test tubes by fertilizing human ova with human sperm. In his original paper entitled "The Human Conceptus During the First Two Weeks of Gestation," he describes the latter as follows: "Another egg similarly treated (with human spermatozoa) began its personal existence by changing from a single cell that has been part of the maternal tissue into a two-cell autonomous structure." Those who recognize the human fetus to be a human being throughout development, and Catholics are numbered among them, will recognize these procedures to be a form of lethal human experimentation.

I mention this early work for only two reasons. First to show that Dr. Rock's intransigence to the teaching of his church dates back at least twenty-five years—a time, incidentally, when the democracies were concerned about dangerously low birth rates resulting from widespread birth control practices, and not, as they are today, about high birth rates in other parts of the world which to some indicate the need for contraception, sterilization, and abortion. Secondly, to show that his intransigence is deeper than one is led to believe by his present urbane speculations on the Church, the contraceptive pill and birth control. His recent prediction in a popular national weekly on the future acceptability of abortions leaves no doubt about his basic convictions: ". . . the dignity of being human," he writes, "can demand of embryos the same responsibility to the preservation of the human race—and hence a willingness to die—that we now demand of soldiers. They go out equally unquestioning, to die on the battlefields for the same purpose."

The notion of a person or the state speaking of human dignity "demanding of" a human embryo who is incapable of expressing his will, "a willingness to die" hardly qualifies as a humanistic position to say nothing of an orthodox Christian position. The analogy of the soldier ignores the valued tradition which respects the conscientious objector and, further, "the God-given conscience" Dr. Rock refers to in his preface. Students of the Nuremberg trials will recognize the danger of courting a position which permits human rights to be compromised. A compromise of human rights is a compromise of the moral order. It was this that seduced the majority of accused German physicians who, in pre-Nazi days, had been "irreproachable citizens happy in their researches or in their professional medical activity."

Dr. Rock has a right to his opinion and its expression. His

bluntness is exemplary. However, since his opinion so clearly departs from the teachings of the faith he espouses and from the teachings of reason unified by the architectonic science of ethics, the basis of most of the Church's moral teaching, it seems misleading to promote the book as "Catholic." It is imperative to differentiate between an individual Catholic's opinion and a Catholic position. Which sensible person would seriously consider as an avant-garde Catholic position the expressed opinion of any Catholic—even a 'devout' priest—were he to proclaim that "the time has come" to recognize white supremacy and the cultural inequality of the colored races advocating that legal, medical and moral action should be taken against blacks, browns, reds and yellows? What can be so easily seen or sensed in racism, however, is not easily seen in contraception.

Despite the difficulty in seeing it, fundamental issues are involved in contraception: the whole order of nature and of love is at stake. It is adolescent to go on thinking of this as merely a matter of condoms and pills. Furthermore, to suspect or penetrate the pitfalls and errors of either racism or contraception, religious faith is not necessary, though God knows it helps.

Dr. Rock's book *Voluntary Parenthood,* co-authored with the Public Information Director of Planned Parenthood and published in 1947, was more appropriately promoted. Then Dr. Rock was characterized, not as a "dedicated Roman Catholic," but simply as a "distinguished physician." The most distressing result of the switch, the decision to trumpet the new book as Catholic, is its confusion of men of good will and its inflammatory effect on men of less than good will. It makes virtually impossible the friendly, intelligent and respectful dialogue vital to our pluralistic society and to a wise solution of our problems.

How difficult this dialogue can become was manifest at a recent Planned Parenthood meeting in Washington honoring Dr. Rock. At that meeting the moderator, the American correspondent for the Manchester *Guardian,* stated, "I'll take bets that in ten years divine guidance will flash down on the Vatican. It will not only be okay to have birth control, it will be compulsory."

This is pretty heady stuff. It has as its thesis and tactic the belief that actual, cultural and/or contrived pressures, exerted on students of God and nature, determine the basic truths that they hold; that truth is exigent, and will bend and snap to public pressure; that theologians and philosophers, both scientists, will respond like politicians. One cannot help but note in passing— with all due respect to serious overpopulation problems and pressing personal problems—that the public clamor for action in the United States is intimately entwined with the middle and upper classes. Their long-standing personal anxieties and problems concerning parenthood are adequately documented. These anxieties have been amplified and rationalized by zealously imposed fears of overpopulation, of outsiders imminently encroaching on their front yard, on their world, and, perhaps, on their conscience.

The clue to understanding Dr. Rock's book lies in his thesis that the Pill is a "natural means of fertility control" and that Pius XII, in condemning oral steroids (the Pill) "on the premise that these are agents which cause 'sterilization'," merely suffered from a semantic difficulty. This portion of the book contains the most tortured thinking concerning a physiologic process and a pharmacologic intervention I have come across in medical literature. We should all be indebted to Dr. Robert E. Hall of Columbia Medical School who, in a review of Dr.

Rock's book in the N. Y. *Times* (May 12, 1963), makes this point with special authority. "Rock's rationalization of the Pill," he writes, "is to me a little short of preposterous. . . . As a birth control enthusiast I would like to dismiss this theory as harmless euphemism; as a doctor I must aver it is medical fantasy." Since Dr. Rock's self-appointed role as a social and religious philosopher is transferred from his medical authority, Dr. Hall's evaluation lends no confidence to Dr. Rock's extended voice.

Dr. Hall's opinion is not an isolated one. At a recent meeting of the Third European Congress of the International Planned Parenthood Federation, a British expert on family planning education from that organization reported on a poll taken of doctors at the World Health Organization: "no single doctor I asked would advise his daughter to use (the Pill)." Similar expressions have been privately reported in this country. At the same meeting, Dr. Nikonchik of the USSR, during a sharp discussion on oral steroid contraceptives, stated that "We have no right to alter the harmonious hormonal structure given by nature." Parenthetically, it should be seen from this that the understanding of rights in God's created order is not limited to those within the Church or to those who only believe in God.

Dr. Rock's candor and authority when it comes to the Pill has the same kind of value as the commercial advertisement of a drug manufacturer, though I think all of us can appreciate the understandably human bias of one talking about his baby. The Pill unquestionably is the most dangerous contraceptive product now on the market. It has caused deaths and heartbreaking medical complications, and its safety is still under investigation by the government. Because of its alleged high acceptance rate by the indigent, a group which has rejected other contraceptives in the past, its dangers are being minimized. This is contributing to the destruction of one of the great traditions of medicine: "that physicians do not prescribe for others, what they will not prescribe for their own."

As one attempts to come to grips with Dr. Rock's thinking on the Pill and population control, it becomes apparent that he has a poor grasp of the order of nature, and following from this, a poor grasp of function in nature. He does not seem to know the meaning of art imitating nature—here one must distinguish between that which occurs naturally and that which occurs according to its nature or basic design. It is this which gives medicine its norms. He does not recognize the work of nature in reproduction as independent from the work of man. He ignores the wisdom of nature—the wisdom which closes the gap between what we know and what we have yet to discover through science. He seems to be indifferent to nature's capacity to strike back. Perhaps he has forgotten the old adage that man sometimes forgives, God always forgives, but nature never forgives. Without an adequate understanding of nature and man, Dr. Rock, in my opinion, is handicapped in seeking the solution of the problem he attacks.

As a result his medical approach to the problem of birth control is emptied of any sensitivity to the nature and mystique of woman, that which flows from her delicate and subtle psychohormonic harmony and her lunar rhythms, that which keeps her in touch with the cosmos and her true self. The Pill, by imposing upon her a continuing state of false pregnancy, flattens her womanliness. An understanding of the classic work of Drs. Benedek and Rubenstein of the Chicago Institute of Psychoanalysis, *The Sexual Cycle in Women: The Relation Between*

Ovarian Function and Psychodynamic Processes, is desperately relevant.

The population question is bound up with deep-seated emotional, social and spiritual problems in both the patient and prescriber—the plannees and the planners. It must be approached with utmost sophistication. We need an awareness of the need to free ourselves from cultural blinders, as well as to protect ourselves from simplist remedies promising quick victories. This not only applies to thinkers who are Catholics and non-Catholics but to *Catholic* thinkers as well.

Dr. Rock's belief that the population problem compares in magnitude with the atomic problem, and his proposals for a crash program in fertility control, should immediately alert us to the cardinal error of our times: that a technological advance guarantees human progress. Let us not repeat the error we made with the atomic bomb of conceiving the problem as primarily technological. Now as then, it is not the discovery of means but a wise use of means to which we should be directing our major attention. We all know in the case of the atomic bomb the suffering our failure of forethought has inflicted upon the world. It would be equally disastrous if, again, for a want of a policy we commit the same mistake in fertility control. It too, in its varied way, could decimate the world.

Consequently, though we welcome and need their specialty contributions, the faster we get the manipulation of population problems out of the hands of obstetricians and demographers, the quicker we will arrive at a sound solution to the problems that confront us. Here we should recall the thought of Francis Bacon concerning the abuse of specialty thinking as an impediment to the advancement of the sciences: "men have used to infect their meditations, opinions, and doctrines, with some conceits which they have most admired, or *some Sciences which they have most applied;* and give all things else a *tincture* according to them *utterly untrue and improper.* . . . So have the alchemists made a philosophy out of a few experiments of the furnace; and Gilbertus . . . a philosophy out of the observations of a lodestone. . . . But of these conceits Aristotle speaketh seriously and wisely when he saith, 'they who contemplate a few things have no difficulty in deciding.' "

VI

The Economics
Of Population

COLIN CLARK

**Can the economic development of the world keep pace
with the growth of an uncontrolled world population?**

*Colin Clark is Director of the Agricultural Economics Re-
search Institute at Oxford University. He has taught at Cambridge, Harvard, the University of Chicago, and the Universities
of Melbourne, Sydney and Western Australia. He has served
on the Economic Advisory Council, Cabinet Offices in London
and was Under-Secretary of State for Labor and Industry, and
Director of the Bureau of Industry and Financial Advisor to
the Treasury in Queensland, Australia. He holds an M.A. degree
in Science from Oxford, M.A. in Economics from Cambridge,
Honorary Doctorates from Milan and Tilburg Universities and
is Council Member of the Royal Statistical Society, Fellow of
the Econometric Society, Member of the French Academy of
Agriculture, and Fellow of Brasenose College, Oxford. This
article appeared in* Pax Romana Journal 2 of 1963.

The case for and against unrestricted population expansion is
often argued conflictingly on religious and economic grounds.
Many people assume that economic considerations indicate that
some limitation of future population growth is desirable and
that those who oppose population restriction do so from reli-

gious conviction. Very few people are fully qualified to argue as experts on both aspects of this problem, though not many realize this, and as a result the facts are often obscured by ill-informed prejudices of one sort or another. This article is not concerned with the moral problems involved, but by carefully considering the economics of this difficult subject, and objectively examining the facts, it is hoped to clear up some misconceptions.

THE HUNGRY "TWO-THIRDS"

In 1950, the journal, *Scientific American,* published an article by Lord Boyd-Orr, a former Director General of the World Food and Agriculture Organization, which focused attention on the rapid growth of world population, and succeeded in arousing considerable interest and anxiety on both sides of the Atlantic. It was this article which first made the disturbing statement that two-thirds of the world's population were forced to endure a lifetime of hunger and malnutrition. The statement received widespread publicity, and has been incorporated in most popular writings on this subject since.

Most present-day discussions of world population problems are based on this gloomy estimate, which was shortly afterwards shown to be inaccurate. The Director of the Food Research Institute at Stanford University, M. K. Bennett, an outstanding authority in this field, has shown in his book, *The World's Food,* how Lord Boyd-Orr's conclusion about two-thirds of the world's population was the result of misunderstanding the nature of a table of statistics compiled by FAO. It would appear to have been the result of confusing target figures for calorie consumption with those for minimum calorie requirements. It must also be pointed out that most of these early estimates by FAO were highly inaccurate in any case.

Subsequent estimates by FAO have painted a less gloomy, if at times a confused, picture. Some time after the publication of Lord Boyd-Orr's "two-thirds" figure, estimates produced by FAO claimed that approximately one-half of the world's population was hungry. Recently, however, the Director of Statistics for FAO, Dr. P. N. Sukhatme, himself an Indian, in a paper read before the Royal Statistical Society in London in May 1961, concluded that about 10 to 15 per cent of the world's population are undernourished. This figure is probably the most realistic assessment of the true position. (It is true that he made some further statements about a further large proportion of the world's population being "malnourished," but as he gave neither definition nor evidence for them, these statements, from the scientific point of view, can be disregarded.)

Communist China probably contains the largest number of hungry people in the world. The amount of calories consumed by a large proportion of the population in pre-Communist China was below requirements standard—and the situation under communism has deteriorated. The collectivization of farming, seen by many as a panacea for poverty among peasant populations, always seems to be followed by a reduction in agricultural output. Stalin's collectivization of Russian agriculture in the '30's is believed to have been responsible, through famine, for the death of at least 5 million people. Because they are living under Communist regimes, a large number of the people suffering from hunger are not in a position to receive aid or help from FAO or any outside agency. The caste system also is one of the principal causes of hunger in India. Though theoretically abolished, this system continues to flourish and means a systematic denial of economic opportunity to a very large section of India's population.

In any consideration of the economics of world population, it must be emphasized from the beginning that the productive capacity of agriculture is not static, but is being constantly improved by the development and application of new techniques to agriculture. The mistaken belief common to most Malthusians, that the amount of land required to support a human being is fixed, or at least capable of only a very limited modification, is at the bottom of many gloomy forecasts.

The widespread abandonment of the caste system in India, for instance, and the introduction of certain basic and practical reforms would enable Indian agriculture to provide a much more satisfactory diet for her present population, and to feed the annual increase of 2 per cent adequately. If India adopted Japanese techniques of cultivation, the agricultural output from the same area of land would be nearly four times that produced at present. After every Indian had eaten his fill, the world would be flooded with a deluge of unsaleable rice.

Population expansion can be a powerful stimulus to growth in all sectors of an economy. It is foolish to think of the discovery and adoption of scientific and technical improvements in industry and agriculture as being events which occur independently, without any external stimulus (apart that is, from the intellectual incentives for scientific experimentation in laboratories.) The Malthusian who believes this is able to reason that, if population growth could be reduced or stopped altogether, these improvements would continue to take place and we would all be proportionately so much better off. He ignores the important role of population pressure in providing a stimulus for the adoption of these technical improvements.

POPULATION CRISES

A study of the history of the economic development of mankind shows that a rapid increase in numbers, by putting a temporary strain on food resources, can act as an effective stimulant for all sorts of developments and changes in a nation's way of life.

The European economy of over 5,000 years ago was based on hunting and fishing. As the growth of population made the available hunting ground inadequate, our ancestors appear to have experienced an economic crisis which led to domestication of animals—for even the most primitive grazing methods will support at least one person per square mile. Agricultural cultivation followed later on. Since the world's oldest known agricultural communities are now known to have been irrigation settlements in the arid climates of Jericho, Egypt and Babylonia, where there is not much grazing land for livestock, it is easy to believe that these people also had strong incentives to experiment with new forms of food production.

The next stage of economic growth is from a rural civilization based on agriculture to an urban civilization based on commerce, and here the ancient Greeks provide us with an interesting example of a people outrunning their agricultural resources and being stimulated by a population crisis to further progress. As early as the 7th century B.C., the Greeks were building commercial cities on uninhabited land all around the Mediterranean—even while the poet Hesiod was bitterly complaining that the country was becoming so overpopulated that everybody would be much poorer in the future. A century or two later, Greek civilization had reached its peak; the country was densely populated, with trade and manufacture as the main occupations of the people. The achievements of the Greeks in cultural and intellectual fields at this time surpass their remarkable economic development. Greek sculpture, architecture, poetry, history, philosophy, mathematics and science laid the essential foundations of the culture and civilization on which we pride ourselves today.

There was probably little net population growth in Europe between the second and the tenth century; in some regions population may have declined in that tumultuous period. On the other hand, in the medieval period, which saw some of the greatest developments and achievements in European civilization, population started to expand rapidly.

In Holland at the beginning of the 17th century, we find another example of how the pressure of population on agricultural resources ultimately led to vigorous developments in the nation's social and economic life. With characteristic stubbornness, on limited resources, the Dutch resisted attempts at domination by one of the greatest military powers of the time, Spain, then proceeded to transform themselves into the foremost commercial and maritime power in the world. As well as founding cities in Africa, America and Indonesia, and discovering Australia, the Dutch established themselves as the outstanding painters and craftsmen of the period.

In Britain, where population had been growing for some time, it became clear by the second half of the 18th century that the increased population could not be supported for long under the existing agricultural system. In 1798, the Reverend Thomas

Malthus, in an "Essay on the Principles of Population," expounded certain ideas which have had a powerful impact on all discussions of population problems ever since. Malthus was worried by the apparent overpopulation of Britain (population 10 million), and by the tendency, which he thought he detected, for human beings to multiply more rapidly than the means of subsistence. Apparently unaware of the developments in agriculture and industrial technology which were occurring in Britain at that time, Malthus felt that this population growth would have to be checked, if population were not to increase beyond the food-producing resources available. He advocated late marriages (not contraception, as is sometimes stated) as the best means of checking this growth of population. Or else, he said, vice and misery would act as a natural check to bring population back within the limits of food-producing resources available.

Malthus underestimated the stimulus provided by population pressure. The early 19th Century saw a radical transformation of society in Britain—economic, political and cultural—in which improved agricultural techniques and industrial development were accompanied by outstanding achievements in science and literature. In addition, the rapid population increase both enabled and encouraged large numbers to emigrate to North America, where they married young, and produced large families. Historians agree that the rapid growth in the numbers of English-speaking people in American at this time is unquestionably the reason why the North American continent is now English rather than French or Spanish-speaking.

Indeed, it is possible to say that if the rapid increase in population in England and Ireland, which began about the middle of the 18th Century, had not occurred, the United States and Australia might never have developed as they are now, and Britain might have remained an unprogressive 18th-century agrarian community without any great degree of industrialization, with the rest of Europe also following her example.

If the warnings of Malthus about unrestricted population growth went unheeded in Britain, they do appear to have had a real following in France, where a decline in the size of families began in the early 19th century. Instead of the increasing prosperity which Malthus expected, the French economy stagnated in the following decades. Professor Sauvy, the leader of the French delegation to the World Population Conference in 1954, made a quite unanswerable statement when he said that, if population restriction were the key to economic growth, France by now, after a century and a half of it, should have become one of the richest countries in the world.

Instead, the lack of incentive among French peasants to improve farming methods, or to seek industrial employment, was responsible for the poor achievements of the French economy in the 19th century. French economic development is now proceeding rapidly, and French economic historians have suggested that this 19th century check to population was largely responsible for France's late start. Apart from economic effects, many Frenchmen believe that this check on population growth has had its effect on their country's political influence in the world, which has been steadily declining from what it was in the late 18th century and early 19th century.

The experience of Japan in the late 19th century provides further evidence of the "take-off" period of a country's economic development being initiated by a rapid increase in population growth. When the Emperor Meiji embarked on a policy of modernization and reform in 1868 the Japanese were far poorer than the inhabitants of most Asian countries are today. Fear of political interference forced him to refuse any foreign aid or financial loans (though he believed in importing the services of foreign teachers and technicians), so Japan had to rely on her own internal resources to produce a long period of economic growth higher and more rapid than that achieved by any other country. All this took place during a period of very rapid population expansion.

Japan's remarkable achievement is all the more interesting when we realize that, apart altogether from the extra food imported in exchange for manufactured exports, the output of food from Japanese agriculture and fisheries was increasing faster than population in spite of the country's extremely limited area of agricultural land. This spectacular increase in food production was caused by a few important technical changes: the selective breeding of higher yielding strains of rice, the use of chemical fertilizers and the motorization of the fishing fleet. One of the most important lessons to be learned from the Japanese experience is that these fundamental improvements could never have been so widely and so thoroughly adopted had it not been for the agrarian and social reforms undertaken by the Emperor at the same time.

The establishment of universal education in 1889, for instance, had very far-reaching consequences. This, as can be well understood, was a very big undertaking for a country as poor as Japan was then. Apart altogether from its inherent value, education has been one of the most important factors, in the long run, in Japan's economic development.

There are good grounds for hoping that what Japan did in the 19th century, India—whose population is now growing rapidly at a rate of 2 per cent per annum—can succeed in doing in the 20th. Indeed, India has many advantages over Japan in starting on a program of economic development. Science and technology have advanced much further today and there is a much better understanding of the problems to be tackled and the improvements to be adopted; the amount of land per head in India is much higher than in Japan; and above all, other foreign countries, particularly the United States, and to a lesser extent, Britain, are giving a large amount of economic aid in the form of both foreign reserves and trained personnel.

The rate of economic progress in India since 1948 has been considerable and, though the figures fluctuate from year to year with variations in harvest, it would appear on average that both agricultural and industrial production in India are growing more rapidly than population.

POPULATION AND ECONOMIC DEVELOPMENT

The common feature of economic development in all these different countries has been the beneficial stimulus they received from the rapid growth in numbers. All these changes have occured after a period when population appeared to be expanding beyond the country's resources—not before. It is probably true that population pressure is the only force powerful enough to overcome the intense conservatism of peasant populations, whether they be Indian, Japanese, British, or Greek. The course of events in France would confirm this. The process of economic growth can be painful for the country concerned if the task of feeding the expanding population puts too great a strain on agricultural resources, and if little help can be got from outside, as happened in Britain in the late 18th and 19th centuries.

In the 1960's, however, most underdeveloped countries seriously embarking on the road to economic advancement, are able to secure technical and financial aid from the wealthier industrial nations. A growing population can be of great economic benefit to a country seeking to build up an industrial sector. An expanding domestic market, able to absorb the increasing output, is a sound basis for developing home production and exports. The large markets necessary to obtain the economies of large-scale production are best assured by a growing population. Statistics of industrial productivity in a number of different countries appear to indicate that the greatest gains in productivity occur in those industries whose market is extending most rapidly. Some considerable harm appears to have been felt by those industrial countries which experienced a check in the growth of their population in recent generations. It is interesting to observe that the average size of family is increasing again in a number of industrial countries, particularly in the United States.

However, to say that population growth benefits a country does not necessarily mean that world population growth is possible for the world as a whole. Everybody knows about the large stocks of surplus food in the United States—obviously the United States could feed a much larger population than it does at present. What about the food and mineral resources of the world as a whole? Is there not a danger that further increases in total world population would exhaust the world's limited agricultural and forest resources?

Many serious minded people are convinced, because of fears of a world food shortage, that there is a sound case on humanitarian grounds for curbing the growth in the world's population which is taking place at present. They fail to realize that the problem is not of a lack of physical resources, but rather a social and economic problem of developing the existing resources carefully, that is, of providing the technical and financial means to exploit the existing potential food supplies.

LAND RESOURCES

We are at present cultivating a good deal less than a third of the land available for cultivation in the world today; and a large part of this is being cultivated by extremely inefficient methods, which, if improved, would produce anything up to a four-fold increase in yield (as in the case of the Indian agriculture mentioned earlier). The largest areas of good uncultivated land are to be found in Africa and Latin America. It is not generally realized just how much good land is lying idle in Asia as well—large parts of Burma, Thailand, two-thirds of Ceylon, nine-tenths of Malaya and almost the whole of Indonesia outside Java are not being used at present. Only in India, Pakistan, Java, parts of Vietnam and China is there any real pressure of population on the land.

The land surface of the world (excluding Greenland and Antarctica), measures 131 million square kilometers. Measurement of the agricultural land available leaves us with the equivalent of 77 million square kilometers of good farm land. (A square kilometer equals 250 acres.)

Of the total land available, 8.6 million square kilometers can be regarded as too cold for agricultural purposes, while 22.6

million consist of arid desert. We will also ignore in our calculations almost all of a further 20 million square kilometers of
semi-arid land, which can in fact be used for grazing and for
occasional agriculture. The rest of the world's land surface is
suitable for cultivation.

Of particular interest here are recent Swedish and Finnish
experiments which have shown that the cold climate country—
a large area of 14.5 million square kilometers, mostly Alaska,
Canada and Soviet Russia—hitherto regarded as unsuitable for
agricultural cultivation, can be made to yield satisfactory har-
vests if required. Of the remaining surface area of the earth,
agriculture output on 7.5 million square kilometers will probably be subject to intermittent crop failure because of sub-humid
climate conditions. If we exclude up to half the area of unusually cold or dry land, but count the 10 million square kilometers of
tropical land with high rainfall twice (because, with proper cultivation this area is capable of yielding two regular crops a
year), we find that the world possesses the equivalent of 77 million square kilometers of good temperate farm land.

The economic significance can be seen from the size of the
population this area could support. In this context, productivity
per unit of land is more important than productivity per man.
In Holland, where agricultural productivity (output per acre of
land) is the highest in Europe, one person's total requirements
for agricultural produce and for timber can be produced from
the equivalent of two-thirds of an acre of land. As well as being
the most productive of European farmers, the Dutch are probably also the healthiest and best fed. If we use Dutch standards
of productivity and also allow their high consumption level, the

world could feed 28 billion people, nearly ten times its present day population. If we care to contemplate a predominantly cereal diet, we could calculate on Japanese standards of productivity and consumption—in which case the agricultural resources of the earth are capable of supporting a population of 92 billion.

These estimates take no account of further improvement in agricultural techniques. But assume that no further technological developments will take place in agriculture (a highly improbable assumption). The possibility of harvesting plants or fish from the sea has also been ignored. Results from agricultural laboratories indicate that ultimately, when we really apply our scientific knowledge to agriculture, a minimum food supply for one person could be got from only 25 square meters of land.

Another argument commonly used by those who wish to limit the growth of world population is that the supply of fuel and minerals would be endangered by any further growth in numbers. Anxiety about the possible exhaustion of the natural supplies of certain metals is groundless. Iron and aluminum are to be found in virtually unlimited deposits all over the globe. Per capita consumption of copper, lead, tin and zinc is falling rapidly as chemists and engineers in advanced industrial countries continue to find new substitutes. Many producers indeed are seriously alarmed by the fall in demand for such minerals.

We need have no anxiety about a future shortage of fuel because we now have or hope shortly to have, nuclear fuels in virtually unlimited quantities. World supplies of crude oil show no signs of being exhausted. Even if the world's entire resources of oil and coal (which can be converted to oil) were to become exhausted, it would still be possible to run motor cars (assuming the automobile to be a form of transport still favored by our descendants) on storage batteries or hydrogen obtained from electrolysis of water by nuclear power.

There is an unfortunate tendency in most discussions of the economics of population growth to ignore the very important fact that the increase in numbers will be accompanied by great increases in economic productivity. Productivity is now increasing in the United States and other industrial countries at a rate sufficient to double productivity in 30 years, and there is no reason to believe that these increases will not continue. (We have seen how, in the history of man's economic development, productivity increases have always been accelerated by population pressure). At this rate, our descendants only three centuries hence—assuming that we have not all been obliterated by some nuclear catastrophe—will be a thousand times more productive than we are.

It seems clear from all this that our duty toward our decendants, both immediate and remote, is not to devise means of effectively preventing their existence, but rather, to use our existing knowledge and techniques to ensure that they will enjoy a higher standard of living than their forebears in many parts of the world today.

VII

Freedom to Die

FRANCIS CANAVAN

Father Canavan, S.J., is an Associate Editor of America, *National Catholic Weekly Review. "Freedom to Die" appeared in the January 11, 1964, issue of* America.

Euthanasia was a hot question in the year 2004. The Euthanasia League was running out of money to operate its sleep havens, as the centers where it performed mercy killings were called. The time had come, it announced, for government to run the havens at public expense.

The proposal got wide support. Taxpayers' groups saw it as a way to cut down the cost of keeping senior citizens alive. A TV program called "The Protectors" proclaimed every man's right to die when he wanted to. Others, even more progressive, added that the community could and should decide when old people on welfare relief and the incurably ill should die. Besides, they said, our rapidly growing population left us no alternative.

As one might have expected, certain religious groups reacted negatively. The U. S. Catholic bishops condemned euthanasia out of hand. A few old-line Protestant bodies and Orthodox Jewish congregations followed suit. But the drift of religious opinion had been for years toward approving euthanasia as a Christian act of mercy.

92

Leading Protestant theologians pointed out that there was not a line in Holy Scripture against mercy killing. Scripture frowned on murder—that much they conceded. But it would be a distortion of the spirit of the Bible, particularly of the New Testament, to take a rigid "thou shalt not," laid down for a primitive people, as applicable to modern society. The law of love, they said, commands us to seek the good of the other in an interpersonal relationship. Love therefore permits—at times even obliges—us to put the other to sleep forever.

A Catholic lady circulated a mimeographed paper around the country, in which she questioned the natural-law argument against euthanasia. What, she asked, could be more natural than dying? And if death is natural, why may we not induce it at will? Man is not bound by mere biology, she said. His essential characteristic is to be existential and to rise above the mechanisms of his physical nature. Man demonstrates the freedom of his nature by asserting his mastery over it. The lady concluded that, far from being a sin against nature, euthanasia was its supreme triumph. A Catholic magazine later published her paper, with a careful explanation that the editors did not intend to advocate mercy killing.

The debate naturally was more advanced in the sophisticated Old World than in the New. A British weekly noted that modern man refused to be bound by the taboos of the Judeo-Christian tradition. Men and women today, it said, were more influenced by the primitive realism of peoples like the Eskimos, whose laudable custom it was to put grandmother out on the ice to freeze to death when she could no longer contribute to the welfare of the family. A London newspaper reported that a visitor to Sweden had seen hardly anyone over 75 years of age there and very few

93

under five. According to the visitor, the Swedes were a happy nation because they had the courage to live by rational modern standards. The *New Statesman* agreed that no modern mind could disapprove of euthanasia. The great danger, it felt, was that the death industry would prove so profitable as a private enterprise that it would become an obstacle to socialism.

Unfortunate incidents constantly arose out of the euthanasia question, especially in America. Catholic intellectuals were distressed and earnestly besought the 43rd session of Vatican Council II to define that the Church was not opposed to euthanasia and never had been. An article appeared simultaneously in *Novena Notes* and the *Partisan Review* exhorting Catholics to stop the fight over mercy killing. The matter even came up as a political issue in the 2004 Presidential campaign. Both candidates sidestepped it by declaring that whatever action they took in regard to euthanasia would be dictated solely by the national interest. But it was becoming clear that such dodges would no longer suffice.

At this juncture the U. S. Supreme Court stepped in with a providential decision. It declared that the constitutional right to life, rightly understood, included the right to death. All laws respecting euthanasia were therefore unconstitutional. Well, no one likes to think he is depriving someone else of his constitutional rights: so Catholic opposition to mercy killing vanished rapidly. Now sociologists report, Catholic grandmothers and grandfathers die just as fast as the older generation among our separated brethren.

Part Three

Mother and Teacher

In 1958, when the anovulant pills were first being rolled, Pope Pius found it necessary to speak somewhat sharply about the enthusiasm of "certain groups of theologians" which revealed "a deviation in moral judgment."

The Holy Father reflected that he was finding himself in the position of another head of the family who more than once had to condemn "moral theologians who were animated by an indiscreet zeal and an ill-judged boldness."

The situation sounds so familiar. *This* could be 1958, except that the ranks of the "certain groups of theologians" have been swelled by certain groups of scientists, demographers, sociologists, clergy, physicians, teachers, and laity in various stages of emergence. And some of them have been courting a pill which itself now seems headed for extinction.

Those few dozen words on periodic continence for the regulation of births which occur in Pius XII, are frequently quoted (apparently as a guarantee of orthodoxy). But here ends any interest in the teachings of Pius XII, in truth very extensive, his predecessors or his successors, with regard to the inestimable value of every new human life. These, somehow can be dismissed as not binding, not relevant, passe, and, to be perfectly frank, just so much flowery verbosity.

95

In the full knowledge that it is absolutely archaic to receive papal directives with love and docility, and that most of us amateurs think we know perfectly well what the Popes have said, I have nevertheless assembled here some of the pertinent passages from modern papal statements. They are a formidable running commentary on almost a century of growing matrimonial chaos and an accurate prophecy, much of it already fulfilled, of the ills to be expected.

These statements are one. They are light shining in the darkness. They are the voice of the true Mother who knows her children, loves them, suffers in their suffering, and endlessly desires their perfection.

Anyone who feels free to pick and choose what he will believe and what not when the Church speaks should consider these words from *Casti Connubii:*

"Let the faithful obey the Church, therefore, if they would keep themselves safe from error and moral corruption. Furthermore, if they are not to deprive themselves of the help so generously provided by God, they must yield their obedience not only to the more solemn definitions of the Church but also, in due measure, to the other constitutions and decrees by which certain opinions are proscribed and condemned as dangerous and vicious.

"So, too, in the questions which are raised at the present day concerning marriage, let the faithful not trust too much in their own judgment or surrender to the allurement of a false freedom or so-called independence of thought.

"It is alien to the true Christian spirit such unweaning confidence in one's own mind as to accept only what one has discovered from a direct examination of the subject; or to restrict one's assent and obedience to the prescriptions laid down in those more solemn definitions above mentioned, as though one might prudently consider the other decisions of the Church to be wrong or insufficiently grounded in truth and moral rectitude. The true Christian, whether learned or unlearned, will allow himself in all matters pertaining to faith and morals to be ruled and guided by the Holy Church of God, through its Supreme Pastor, the Roman Pontiff, who himself is guided by Our Lord Jesus Christ."

1. Leo XIII

These words were applied specifically to the permanence and holiness of marriage which were coming under attack at that time. They are no less applicable to the fecundity of marriage, the aspect most threatened in our day.

From the beginning of the world, indeed, it was divinely ordained that things instituted by God and by Nature should prove to be the more profitable and salutary the more they remain unchanged in their full integrity. For God, the Maker of all things, well knowing what was good for the institution and preservation of each of his creatures, so ordered them by his will and mind that each might adequately attain the end for which it was made. If the rashness or the weakness of men ventures to change or disturb the order of things most providently instituted, then designs of the greatest wisdom and usefulness begin either to be hurtful or cease to be profitable—either because through the change undergone they have lost their power of benefiting, or because God chooses to inflict punishment on the pride and audacity of men.

* * *

But now there is a growing wish to supplant natural and divine law by human law; and hence has begun a gradual extinction of that most excellent ideal of marriage which Nature herself had impressed on the soul of man, and sealed, as it were, with her own seal; nay, even more, even in Christian marriages this power, productive of so great good, has been weakened by the sinfulness of man. [Encyclical—*Arcanum Divinae Sapientiae 2/10/ 1880* Excerpts.]

98

2. *Pius XI*

By the time of Pius XI, the birth control movement had been added to ills affecting marriage. Reaffirming the Church's teaching on the sacredness and permanence of marriage, Pius also defined abuses of the procreative act. "Our intervention," he said, "is not only opportune and necessary, but even urgent." Casti Connubii was a work of "such gravity and importance," that it "demanded long meditation and preparation."

EVILS OPPOSED TO THE BLESSING OF OFFSPRING

Turning now, Venerable Brethren, to treat in detail the vices which are contrary to each of the blessings of matrimony. We must begin with the consideration of offspring, which many nowadays have the effrontery to call a troublesome burden of wedlock—a burden which they urge married folk carefully to avoid, not by means of a virtuous continence (which is permissible even in marriage with the consent of both parties) but by vitiating the act of nature. This criminal abuse is claimed as a right by some on the ground that they cannot endure children, but want to satisfy their carnal desire without incurring any responsibility. Others plead that they can neither observe continence, nor, for personal reasons or for reasons affecting the mother, or on account of economic difficulties, can they consent to have children.

But no reason whatever, even the gravest, can make what is intrinsically against nature become conformable with nature and morally good. The conjugal act is of its very nature designed for the procreation of offspring; and therefore those who in performing it deliberately deprive it of its natural power and efficacy, act against nature and do something which is shameful and intrinsically immoral.

We cannot wonder, then, if we find evidence in the Sacred Scriptures that the Divine Majesty detests this unspeakable crime with the deepest hatred and has sometimes punished it with death, as St. Augustine observes: "Sexual intercourse even with a lawful wife is unlawful and shameful if the conception of offspring is prevented. This is what Onan, the son of Juda, did, and on that account God put him to death."[1]

THE CHRISTIAN TEACHING

Wherefore, since there are some who, openly departing from the Christian teaching which has been handed down uninterruptedly from the beginning, have in recent times thought fit solemnly to preach another doctrine concerning this practice, the Catholic Church, to whom God has committed the task of teaching and preserving morals and right conduct in their integrity, standing erect amidst this moral devastation, raises her voice in sign of her divine mission to keep the chastity of the marriage contract unsullied by this ugly stain, and through Our mouth proclaims anew: that any use of matrimony whatsoever in the exercise of which the act is deprived, by human interference, of its natural power to procreate life, is an offense against the law of God and of nature, and that those who commit it are guilty of a grave sin.

RESPONSIBILITY OF CONFESSORS

Therefore, priests who hear confessions and others who have the care of souls are admonished by Us, in the exercise of Our

---

1. St. Augustine, De conjug. adult., 1. 2, n. 12

sovereign authority and Our care for the salvation of the souls of all, that they must not allow the souls committed to their charge to be in error concerning this most serious law of God, and, what is much more important, that they must themselves be on their guard against these false doctrines and in no way connive at them. Should any confessor or pastor of souls himself—which God forbid—lead into error the faithful committed to his care, or at least, by his approval or by a misleading silence, confirm them in holding such doctrines, then let him know that he will have to render to God, the Sovereign Judge, a strict account of this betrayal of his trust; and he must consider as addressed to himself the words of Christ: "They are blind and leaders of the blind; and if the blind lead the blind, both fall into the pit."[2]

Frequently the motives alleged in defense of the illicit use of marriage are—to say nothing of those that are shameful—fictitious and exaggerated. Nevertheless the Church, who is a loving Mother, hears with sympathetic understanding the plea urged for the ailing mother whose very life may be endangered. Who can fail to be moved with pity at such a thought? And who can refuse a tribute of the highest admiration for the mother who with heroic courage exposes herself to almost certain death in order to preserve the life of the child she has conceived? The sufferings which she has endured in order completely to discharge her natural duty, God alone out of His rich and bountiful mercy can reward; and He will do so most surely with full measure and overflowing.[3]

Holy Church is also well aware that in many cases one of the partners is more sinned against than sinning, reluctantly allow-

---

2. Matt. 15, 14
3. Luke 6, 38

ing a perversion of right order for a truly grave reason. Such a partner is guiltless, so long as the law of charity even then is remembered, and every effort made to dissuade and prevent the other partner from sin. Nor are husband and wife to be accused of acting against nature if they make use of their right in a proper and natural manner, even though natural causes (due to circumstances of time or to certain defects) render it impossible for new life to originate. Both matrimony and the use of the matrimonial right have secondary ends—such as mutual help, the fostering of reciprocal love, and the abatement of concupiscence—which husband and wife are quite entitled to have in view, so long as the intrinsic nature of that act, and therefore its due subordination to its primary end, is safeguarded.

MEETING DIFFICULTIES

We feel deep sympathy also with the unfortunate condition of married persons who for reasons of extreme poverty experience the greatest difficulty in rearing children.

But external conditions, however calamitous, must not be allowed to provide occasion for an error more calamitous still. No difficulty that arises can ever detract from the binding obligation of divine commandments which forbid acts intrinsically evil; there are no circumstances in which husband and wife are unable, with the strength given by God's grace, to discharge their duty faithfully and preserve their chastity in the married state from this shameful stain. This is a truth of faith proclaimed by the teaching authority of the Council of Trent: "Let no man make the rash assertion, condemned by the Fathers, that it is impossible for a man in the state of grace to observe God's commandments. God does not command the impossible. When

He lays a command upon you He bids you do what you are able, and pray for what is beyond your power; and He helps you to have it in your power."[4] [Encyclical—*Casti Connubii, 12/31/30.* Excerpts]

---

4. Council of Trent, sess. 6, c. 11

3. Pius XII

"During the first weeks of his remarkable Pontificate," wrote the compilers of Dear Newlyweds, *"Pius XII innovated the practice of receiving newly-married couples from all walks of life who sought his Apostolic Benediction on their marriages. In spite of the personal distress and deadly crises which beset him before and after the outbreak of World War II, the Pope obviously enjoyed meeting these young people and devoted extraordinary care to the brief talks which he prepared for them. By 1944, when overwhelming demands upon his strength and time finally forced their discontinuance, the seventy-nine discourses of Pius XII to his 'dear newlyweds' constituted a body of counsel, guidance, and encouragement on marriage and family life unique in papal history . . . His unusual ability to communicate affection and understanding was enhanced by a lively and engaging personality, rare gifts of oratory, a towering intellect, and an indefinable air of sanctity. These elements combined to give his words an attractiveness and intensity which cannot be imagined."*

No one who in any sense is committed to matrimony ought to deprive himself, or those entrusted to his care, of the smallest part of this masterwork, Dear Newlyweds. *Against that background of loving contact with families and sensitivity to their needs and aspirations and problems are set the more formal pronouncements which are included here.*

When one thinks of this admirable collaboration of the parents, of nature and of God, from which is born a new human being in the image and likeness of God, (Gen. 1,26-27) how can the precious contribution which you give to such a work be not appreciated? The heroic mother of the Machabees admonished her children: "I know not how you were formed in my womb, for I neither gave you breath, nor soul, nor life, neither did I frame the limbs of every one of you. But the Creator of the world that formed the nativity of men ...". (2 Mac. 7,22)

Therefore, he who approaches this cradle of life's origin and exercises his action in one way or another must know the order which the Creator wishes maintained and the laws which govern it. For here it is not a case of purely physical or biological laws which blind forces and irrational agents obey, but of laws whose execution and effects are entrusted to the voluntary and free cooperation of man.

Unfortunately, cases are not rare in which it is sufficient only to hint at the fact that children are a "blessing" to provoke contradiction and even derision. More often in word and thought the idea of the great "burden" of children is predominant. Inasmuch as this mentality is opposed to God's plan and to Scripture, so is it also contrary to sane reason and the sentiments of nature! If there are conditions and circumstances in which parents without violating God's law can avoid the "blessing" of children, nevertheless these unavoidable and exceptional cases do not authorize anyone to pervert ideas, to despise values and to treat with contempt the mother who had the courage and honor to give life.

THE MOTHER'S DUTIES

One of the fundamental demands of the true moral order is that to the use of the marriage rights there corresponds the sincere internal acceptance of the function and duties of motherhood.

When husband and wife value and appreciate the honor of producing a new life, whose coming they await with holy impatience, your part is a very easy one: it is easy enough to cultivate in them this interior sentiment: the readiness to welcome and cherish that nascent life follows spontaneously. This is unfortunately not always the case; often the child is not wanted; worse still, it is dreaded. How can there be a ready response to the call of duty in such conditions? Your apostolate must in this case be exercised both efficiently and efficaciously: first of all, negatively, by refusing any immoral cooperation; secondly, positively, by turning your delicate care to the task of removing those preconceived ideas, various fears or faint excuses, to removing as far as possible the obstacles, even if external, which may make the acceptance of motherhood painful.

STERILIZATION

It would be more than a mere lack of readiness in the service of life if an attack made by man were to concern not only a single act but should affect the organism itself to deprive it, by means of sterilization, of the faculty of procreating a new life. Here, too, you have a clear rule in the Church's teaching to guide your behavior both interiorly and exteriorly. Direct sterilization—that is, whose aim tends as a means or as an end at making procreation impossible—is a grave violation of the moral law and therefore unlawful. Not even public authority has any right, under the pretext of any "indication" whatsoever, to permit it, and less still to prescribe it or to have it used to the detriment of innocent human beings. This principle is already proclaimed in the above mentioned Encyclical of Pius XI on marriage. Thus, when ten years or so ago sterilization came to be more widely applied, the Holy See saw the necessity of expressly and publicly declaring that direct sterilization, either perpetual or temporary, in either the male or the female, is unlawful according to natural law, from which, as you well know, not even the Church has the power to dispense.

As far as you can, oppose, in your apostolate, these perverse tendencies and do not give them your cooperation.

BIRTH CONTROL

Today, besides, another grave problem has arisen, namely, if and how far the obligation of being ready for the service of maternity is reconcilable with the ever more general recourse to the periods of natural sterility (the so-called "agenesic" periods in woman), which seems a clear expression of a will contrary to that precept.

It is necessary first of all to consider two hypotheses. If the application of that theory implies that husband and wife may use their matrimonial right even during the days of natural sterility no objection can be made. In this case they do not hinder or jeopardize in any way the consummation of the natural act and its ulterior natural consequences. It is exactly in this that the application of the theory, of which We are speaking, differs essentially from the abuse already mentioned, which consists in the perversion of the act itself. If, instead, husband and wife go further, that is, limiting the conjugal act exclusively to those periods, then their conduct must be examined more closely.

Here again we are faced with two hypotheses. If one of the parties contracted marriage with the intention of limiting the matrimonial right itself to the periods of sterility, and not only its use, in such a manner that during the other days the other party would not even have the right to ask for the debt, then this would imply an essential defect in the marriage consent, which would result in the marriage being invalid, because the right deriving from the marriage contract is a permanent, uninterrupted and continuous right of husband and wife with respect to each other.

However if the limitation of the act to the periods of natural sterility does not refer to the right itself but only to the use of the right, the validity of the marriage does not come up for discussion. Nonetheless, the moral lawfulness of such conduct of husband and wife should be affirmed or denied according as their intention to observe constantly those periods is or is not based on sufficiently morally sure motives. *The mere fact that husband and wife do not offend the nature of the act* and are even ready to accept and bring up the child, who, notwithstanding their precautions, might be born, *would not be itself sufficient to guarantee the rectitude of their intention* and the unobjectionable morality of their motives.

The reason is that marriage obliges the partners to a state of life, which even as it confers certain rights so it also imposes the accomplishment of a positive work concerning the state itself. In such a case, the general principle may be applied that a positive action may be omitted if grave motives, independent of the good will of those who are obliged to perform it, show that its performance is inopportune, or prove that it may not be claimed with equal right by the petitioner—in this case, mankind.

The matrimonial contract, which confers on the married couple the right to satisfy the inclination of nature, constitutes them in a state of life, namely, the matrimonial state. Now, on married couples, who make use of the specific act of their state, nature and the Creator impose the function of providing for the preservation of mankind. This is the characteristic service which gives rise to the peculiar value of their state, the *bonum prolis*. The individual and society, the people and the State, the Church itself, depend for their existence, in the order established by God, on fruitful marriages. Therefore, to embrace the matrimonial state, to use continually the faculty proper to such a state and lawful only therein, and, at the same time, to avoid its primary duty without a grave reason, would be a sin against the very nature of married life.

Serious motives, such as those which not rarely arise from medical, eugenic, economic and social so-called "indications," may exempt husband and wife from the obligatory, positive debt for a long period or even for the entire period of matrimonial life. From this it follows that the observance of the natural sterile periods may be *lawful*, from the moral viewpoint: and it is lawful in the conditions mentioned. If, however, according to a reasonable and equitable judgment, there are no such grave reasons either personal or deriving from exterior circumstances, the will to avoid the fecundity of their union, while continuing to satisfy to the full their sensuality, can only be the result of a false appreciation of life and of motives foreign to sound ethical principles.

THE HEROISM OF CONTINENCE

Perhaps you will now press the point, however, observing that in the exercise of your profession you find yourselves sometimes faced with delicate cases, in which, that is, there cannot be a demand that the risk of maternity be run, a risk which in certain cases must be absolutely avoided, and in which as well the observance of the agenesic periods either does not give sufficient security, or must be rejected for other reasons. Now, you ask, how can one still speak of an apostolate in the service of maternity?

If, in your sure and experienced judgment, the circumstances require an absolute "no," that is to say, the exclusion of motherhood, it would be a mistake and a wrong to impose or advise a "yes." Here it is a question of basic facts and therefore not a theological but a medical question; and thus it is in your competence. However, in such cases, the married couple does not desire a medical answer, of necessity a negative one, but seeks an approval of a "technique" of conjugal activity which will not give rise to maternity. And so you are again called to exercise your apostolate inasmuch as you leave no doubt whatsoever that even in these extreme cases *every preventive practice* and every direct attack upon the life and the development of the seed is, in conscience, forbidden and excluded, and that there is only one way open, namely, to abstain from every complete performance of the natural faculty. Your apostolate in this matter requires that you have a clear and certain judgment and a calm firmness.

It will be objected that such an abstention is impossible, that such a heroism is asking too much. You will hear this objection raised; you will read it everywhere. Even those who should be in a position to judge very differently, either by reason of their duties or qualifications, are ever ready to bring forward the following argument: "No one is obliged to do what is impossible, and it may be presumed that no reasonable legislator can will his law to oblige to the point of impossibility. But for husbands and wives long periods of abstention are impossible. Therefore they are not obliged to abstain; divine law cannot have this meaning."

In such a manner, from partially true premises, one arrives at a false conclusion. To convince oneself of this it suffices to invert the terms of the argument: "God does not oblige anyone to do what is impossible. But God obliges husband and wife to abstinence if their union cannot be completed according to the laws of nature. Therefore in this case abstinence is possible." To confirm this argument, there can be brought forward the doctrine of the Council of Trent, which, in the chapter on the observance necessary and possible of the commandments, referring to a passage of St. Augustine, teaches: "God does not command the impossible, but while He commands, He warns you to do what you can and to ask for the grace for what you cannot do, and He helps you so that you may be able."

Do not be disturbed, therefore, in the practice of your profession and apostolate, by this great talk of impossibility. Do not be disturbed in your internal judgment nor in your external conduct. Never lend yourselves to anything which is contrary to the law of God and to your Christian conscience! It would be a wrong towards men and women of our age to judge them incapable of continuous heroism. Nowadays, for many a reason,—perhaps constrained by dire necessity or even at times oppressed by injustice—heroism is exercised to a degree and to an extent that in the past would have been thought impossible. Why, then, if circumstances truly demand it, should this heroism stop at the limits prescribed by the passions and the inclinations of nature? It is clear: he who does not want to master himself is not able to do so, and he who wishes to master himself relying only upon his own powers, without sincerely and perseveringly seeking divine help, will be miserably deceived.

THE ORDER OF VALUES

"Personal values" and the need to respect such are a theme

which, over the last twenty years or so, has been considered more and more by writers. In many of their works, even the specifically sexual act has its place assigned, that of serving the "person" of the married couple. The proper and most profound sense of the exercise of conjugal rights would consist in this, that the union of bodies is the expression and the realization of personal and affective union.

Articles, chapters, entire books, conferences, especially dealing with the "technique" of love, are composed to spread these ideas, to illustrate them with advice to the newly married as a guide in matrimony, in order that they may not neglect, through stupidity or a false sense of shame or unfounded scruples, that which God, Who also created natural inclinations, offers them. If from their complete reciprocal gift of husband and wife there results a new life, it is a result which remains outside, or, at the most, on the border of "personal values"; a result which is not denied, but neither is it desired as the center of marital relations.

Now, if this relative evaluation were merely to place the emphasis on the personal values of husband and wife rather than on that of the offspring, it would be possible, strictly speaking, to put such a problem aside. But, however, it is a matter of a grave inversion of the order of values and of the ends imposed by the Creator Himself. We find Ourselves faced with the propagation of a number of ideas and sentiments directly opposed to the clarity, profundity, and seriousness of Christian thought. Here, once again, the need for your apostolate. It may happen that you receive the confidences of the mother and wife and are questioned on the more secret desires and intimacies of married life. How, then, will you be able, aware of your mission, to give weight to truth and right order in the appreciation and action of the married couple, if you yourselves are not furnished with the strength of character needed to uphold what you know to be true and just?

THE PRIMARY END OF MARRIAGE

Now, the truth is that matrimony, as an institution of nature, in virtue of the Creator's will, has not as a primary and intimate end the personal perfection of the married couple but the procreation and upbringing of new life. The other ends, inasmuch as they are intended by nature, are not equally primary, much less superior to the primary end, but are essentially subordinated to it. This is true of every marriage, even if no offspring result; just as of every eye it can be said that it is destined and formed to see, even if, in abnormal cases arising from special internal or external conditions, it will never be possible to achieve visual perception.

It was precisely to end the uncertainties and deviations which threatened to diffuse errors regarding the scale of values of the purposes of matrimony and of their reciprocal relations, that a few years ago (March 10, 1944)[1], We Ourselves drew up a declaration on the order of those ends, pointing out what the very internal structure of the natural disposition reveals. We showed what has been handed down by Christian tradition, what the Supreme Pontiffs have repeatedly taught, and what was then in due measure promulgated by the Code of Canon Law.[2] Not long afterwards, to correct opposing opinions, the Holy See, by a public decree, proclaimed that it could not admit the opin-

---

1. It seems as though this declaration was not published, but it must have been similar to the Decree of the Holy Office quoted here above. (Cf. *De re matrimoniali*, Romae, *apud aedes Pont. Universitatis Gregorianae,* 1951, p. 424, 30).

2. C.I.C., can. 1013, §1.

ion of some recent authors who denied that the primary end of marriage is the procreation and education of the offspring, or teach that the secondary ends are not essentially subordinated to the primary end, but are on an equal footing and independent of it.[3]

Would this lead, perhaps, to Our denying or diminishing what is good and just in personal values resulting from matrimony and its realization? Certainly not, because the Creator has designed that for the procreation of a new life human beings made of flesh and blood, gifted with soul and heart, shall be called upon as men and not as animals deprived of reason to be the authors of their posterity. It is for this end that the Lord desires the union of husband and wife. Indeed, the Holy Scripture says of God that He created man to His image and He created him male and female, and willed—as is repeatedly affirmed in Holy Writ—that "a man shall leave mother and father, and shall cleave to his wife: and they shall be two in one flesh."

All this is therefore true and desired by God. But, on the other hand, it must not be divorced completely from the primary function of matrimony—the procreation of offspring. Not only the common work of external life, but even all personal enrichment—spiritual and intellectual—all that in married love as such is most spiritual and profound, has been placed by the will of the Creator and of nature at the service of posterity. The per-

---

3. Sacred Congregation of the Holy Office, 1st April 1944; AAS 36 (1944) 103. Dez. n. 2295:
   —To the query: "Is it possible to admit the opinion of some authors who deny that the primary end of matrimony is the procreation and education of the offspring, or teach that the secondary ends are not essentially subordinated to the primary ends, but are with them parallel *(aeque principales)* and independent?" the Holy Office decreed: *"It cannot be admitted."* This reply, given on the 29th March, 1944, was approved by H.H. Pope Pius XII on the 30th March, 1944 and published on April 1st, of the same year.

fect married life, of its very nature, also signifies the total devotion of parents to the well-being of their children, and married love in its power and tenderness is itself a condition of the sincerest care of the offspring and the guarantee of its realization.

Advise the fiancée or the young married woman who comes to seek your advice about the values of matrimonial life that these personal values, both in the sphere of the body and the senses and in the sphere of the spirit, are truly genuine, but that the Creator has placed them not in the first, but in the second degree of the scale of values.

To these considerations must be added another which tends to be forgotten. All these secondary values of the procreative sphere and activity are included in the ambit of the specific function of husband and wife, which is to be authors and educators of a new life. A high and noble duty! Yet one which does not pertain to the essence of a complete human being, because, if the natural generative tendency does not come to its realization, there is no diminution of the human person, in any way or degree. The renunciation of this realization is not—especially if made for more sublime purposes—a mutilation of personal and spiritual values. Of such free renunciation for the love of God's kingdom the Lord has said: *"Non omnes capiunt verbum istud, sed quibus datum est*—Not all can accept this teaching; but to those to whom it has been given". (Matt. 19, 11)

To exalt beyond measure, as it is often done today, the generative function, even in the just and moral form of married life, is therefore not only an error and an aberration; it also bears with itself the danger of intellectual and affective error, capable of preventing and stifling good and lofty sentiments, especially in youth which is still without experience and ignorant of life's delusions. For what normal man, healthy in body and soul, would like to belong to the number of those deficient in character and spirit?

May your apostolate enlighten the minds and inculcate in them this just order of values, there where you exercise your profession, so that men may conform to it in their judgments and conduct!

HUMAN DIGNITY IN THE CONJUGAL ACT

This explanation of Ours on the functions of your professional apostolate would be incomplete, if We did not add further a few words about the defense of human dignity in the use of the pro-creative faculty.

The same Creator, Who in His bounty and wisdom willed to make use of the work of man and woman, by uniting them in matrimony, for the preservation and propagation of the human race, has also decreed that in this function the parties should experience pleasure and happiness of body and spirit. Husband and wife, therefore, by seeking and enjoying this pleasure do no wrong whatever. They accept what the Creator has destined for them.

Nevertheless, here also, husband and wife must know how to keep themselves within the limits of a just moderation. As with the pleasure of food and drink so with the sexual act they must not abandon themselves without restraint to the impulses of the senses. The right rule is this: the use of the natural procreative disposition is morally lawful in matrimony only, in the service of and in accordance with the ends of marriage itself. Hence it follows that only in marriage with the observing of this rule is

116

the desire and fruition of this pleasure and of this satisfaction lawful. For the pleasure is subordinate to the law of the action whence it derives, and not vice versa—the action to the law of pleasure. And this law, so very reasonable, concerns not only the substance but also the circumstances of the action, so that, even when the substance of the act remains morally safe, it is possible to sin in the way it is performed.

The transgression of this law is as old as original sin. But in our times there is the risk that one may lose sight of the fundamental principle itself. At present, in fact, it is usual to support in words and in writing (and this by Catholics in certain circles) the necessary autonomy, the proper end, and the proper value of sexuality and of its realization, independently of the purpose of procreating a new life. There is a tendency to subject to a new examination and to a new norm the very order established by God and not to admit any other restraint to the way of satisfying the instinct than by considering the essence of the instinctive act. In addition there would be substituted a license to serve blindly and without restraint the whims and instincts of nature in the place of the moral obligations to dominate passions; and this sooner or later cannot but turn out to be a danger to morals, conscience and human dignity.

If nature had aimed exclusively, or at least in the first place, at a reciprocal gift and possession of the married couple in joy and delight, and if it had ordered that act only to make happy in the highest possible degree their personal experience, and not to stimulate them to the service of life, then the Creator would have adopted another plan in forming and constituting the natural act. Now, instead, all this is subordinated and ordered to that unique, great law of the *"generatio et educatio prolis,"*

117

namely the accomplishment of the primary end of matrimony as the origin and source of life.

Unfortunately, unceasing waves of hedonism invade the world and threaten to submerge in the swelling tide of thoughts, desires and acts the whole marital life, not without serious dangers and grave prejudice to the primary duty of husband and wife.

There are some who would allege that happiness in marriage is in direct proportion to the reciprocal enjoyment in conjugal relations. It is not so: indeed, happiness in marriage is in direct proportion to the mutual respect of the partners, even in their intimate relations; not that they regard as immoral and refuse what nature offers and what the Creator has given, but because this respect, and the mutual esteem which it produces, is one of a pure love, and for this reason all the more tender.

In the performance of your profession, do your utmost to repel the attack of this refined hedonism void of spiritual values and thus unworthy of Christian married couples. Show how nature has given, truly, the instinctive desire for pleasure and sanctions it in the lawful marriage, not as an end in itself, but rather for the service of life. Banish from your heart that cult of pleasure, and do your best to prevent the spreading of a literature which considers as its duty the description in full of the intimacies of married life under the pretext of instructing, guiding and reassuring. In general, common sense, natural instinct and a brief instruction on the clear and simple maxims of Christian moral law, are sufficient to give peace to the tender conscience of married people. If, in certain circumstances, a fiancée or a young married woman were in need of further enlightenment on some particular point, it is your duty to give them tactfully an explanation in conformity with natural law and with a healthy Christian conscience.

This teaching of Ours has nothing to do with Manichaeism and Jansenism, as some would have people believe in order to justify themselves. It is only a defense of the honor of Christian matrimony and of the personal dignity of the married couple. [*The Laws of Conjugal Relations.* All. to midwives, 10/29/51. Excerpts.]

LAWFUL METHOD OF CONTROLLING BIRTHS

The Church, on the other hand, can understand with sympathy and comprehension, the real difficulties of matrimonial life in these our days. For this reason, in Our last address on conjugal morality (All. to the midwives), we affirmed the legitimacy and at the same time the limits—truly very wide—of that controlling of births which, unlike the so-called "birth control," is compatible with God's law. It can be hoped (but in such matters the Church naturally leaves the judgment to medical science) that for such a lawful method a sufficiently certain basis can be found, and recent research seems to confirm this hope.

AID IN THE TRIALS OF CONJUGAL LIFE

To overcome the many trials of conjugal life there is above all the most powerful aid of a lively Faith and a frequenting of the Sacraments whence emerge torrents of strength whose efficacy is hardly clearly known by those who are outside of the Church. We wish to close Our speech by recalling these sublime aids. It may also happen to you, beloved sons and daughters, that one day or another, you may feel your courage being troubled by the violent storm raging about you, and, even more dangerously, in the midst of your family, by the doctrines which subvert the wholesome and normal concept of Christian marriage. Be trustful: Nature's energies and, above all, those of grace with which God has enriched your souls by the means of the Sacrament of matrimony are like a solid rock, against which the waves of a stormy sea break up powerless. . . . [*Respect for Life.* All. to Association of Large Families, 11/26/51. Excerpts.]

ON POPULATION

We certainly won't deny the fact that this or that country is at present burdened by relative overpopulation. But wishing to escape from embarrassment by using the formula that the number of inhabitants must be regulated according to the public economy is equivalent to upsetting the order of nature and the whole psychological and moral world with which it is bound up. What an error it would be to blame the natural laws for the present anxieties, when it is obvious that these derive from the lack of solidarity between men and people themselves! [*Mechanized Society,* Radio Message to the World 12/24/52. Excerpt.]

* * *

The science of population is young, but it is basic since it touches immediately on human life and it can clarify some of the most serious individual and social problems.

The Church is not ignorant of these problems; it is not indifferent to their anguishing aspects, as is evidenced by the many documents which have been issued recently by the Holy See on family life, national economy, and the relations between peoples, some of whom find themselves abundantly furnished with riches, while others remain in tragic conditions.

But the Church has always wanted to place the problems of population in their true perspective; that of a moral, personal destiny, which through courageous and even daring action in time, is to find its accomplishment in the eternal possession of God.

That is why We can only rejoice at the light that your labors and those of all sincere population experts bring to the knowledge of the laws and the values which condition the development of population. That is why we are also urging Catholics to take an active part in the researches and in the efforts which are being made in this field. But We want them to do it with fidelity to Christian doctrine, in communion with the many men and women who, enlightened by their reason and sustained by a proper confidence in Providence, fully conscious of the difficulties which they are facing and of their duties toward the community, respect the creative vow which is to be found at the very heart of love and of life. [Message to Catholic Members of World Congress on Population. 9/9/54.]

PERSONAL INTEREST SUBORDINATED TO PARENTHOOD

Several times it has been necessary for Us to recall how the peculiar intentions of the married couple, their life in common, their personal perfection, cannot be conceived unless they are subordinated to the primary end, namely fatherhood and motherhood . . . This is the constant teaching of the Church. She has rejected all those concepts of matrimony which threatened to enfold it in itself or to make it an egoistic search for affective and physical satisfaction in the sole interest of husband and wife.

BIOLOGICAL ACTIVITY AND PERSONAL RELATIONSHIP INSEPARABLE

But the Church has likewise rejected the opposite attitude

which pretended to separate, in procreation, the biological activity from the personal relations of husband and wife. The child is the fruit of the marriage union, when it finds full expression by the placing in action of the functional organs, of the sensible emotions thereto related, and of the spiritual and disinterested love which animates such a union; it is in the unity of this human act that there must be considered the biological conditions of procreation. Never is it permitted to separate these different aspects to the point of excluding positively either the intention of procreation or the conjugal relation.

HUMAN FERTILITY VESTED WITH MORAL ASPECTS

The relation which unites mother and father to their child is rooted in the organic fact, and further still in the deliberate action of husband and wife, who give themselves one to the other and whose will to surrender themselves is revealed and finds its true result in the being they bring into the world. Only this consecration of self, generous in its principle and arduous in its realization, with the conscientious acceptance of the responsibilities it carries, can guarantee that the work of educating the children will be followed with all the diligence, courage and patience required. It can therefore be affirmed that human fertility, beyond the physical plane, is vested with essentially moral aspects which must be considreed, even when this question is treated from the medical viewpoint. [Allocution to Members of II World Congress of Fertility and Sterility 5-19-56. Excerpts.]

The Large Family

An Address of Pope Pius XII to the Directors of
the Associations for Large Families of Rome and of Italy
January 20, 1958

Beloved sons and daughters, Officers and Representatives of the Associations for Large Families of Rome and of Italy, this visit of yours has to be listed among those that bring deepest pleasure to Our heart.

You are well aware of the lively interest We have in family life, of how We never miss an opportunity to point out its many-sided dignity, to re-assert its rights and defend them, to inculcate the duties it involves—in a word, We make it a key-point of Our pastoral teaching.

It is this same anxious interest in families that makes Us agree so readily to spend at least a few moments with family groups that come to Our home (whenever the duties of Our office do not make this impossible), and this is why, on occasion, We consent to be photographed in the midst of them, so as to leave some kind of lasting record of Our joy and theirs.

FATHER OF THE HUMAN FAMILY

The Pope in the midst of a family! Isn't that right where he belongs? Isn't he (in the loftiest spiritual sense of the word) the *Father* of the whole human family that has been reborn in Christ and in the Church? Is it not through him, the Vicar of Christ on earth, that the wonderful plan of creative Wisdom is put into effect—a plan that has conferred on all human father-

123

hood the destiny of preparing a chosen family for heaven, where the love of the One and Triune God will enfold them in a single eternal embrace and give them Himself as the inheritance that will make them perfectly happy?

A TRIPLE TESTIMONY

But you do not represent just any families at all; you are and represent large families, those most blessed by God and specially loved and prized by the Church as its most precious treasures. For these families offer particularly clear testimony to three things that serve to assure the world of the truth of the Church's doctrine and the soundness of its practice, and that redound, through good example, to the great benefit of all other families and of civil society itself.

Wherever you find large families in great numbers, they point to: the physical and moral health of a Christian people; a living faith in God and trust in His Providence; the fruitful and joyful holiness of Catholic marriage.

We would like to say a few words about each of these points.

I

Surely, one of the most harmful aberrations that has appeared in modern society with its pagan tendencies is the opinion of those who are eager to classify fruitfulness in marriage as a "social malady," and who maintain that any nation that finds itself thus afflicted must exert every effort and use every means to cure the disease. This is the basis for the propaganda that goes under the name of "planned parenthood"; at times it is promoted by persons and organizations who command respect because of their positions in other fields, but who, unfortunately, have taken a stand in this matter which must be condemned.

BIRTH CONTROL

Sad as it is to realize how widespread doctrines and practices of this kind have become, even among the traditionally healthy classes, it is comforting to see indications and proofs of a healthy reaction in your country, both in the legal and in the medical fields. As you know, article 31 of the current Constitution of the Italian Republic, to cite just one source, pays "special attention to large families," and the prevailing teaching among Italian doctors is along a line of opposition ever more strongly against birth-control practices.

This does not mean that the danger has passed and that we have destroyed the prejudices which tend to make marriage and its wise norms submit to the aims of reprehensible pride and selfishness on the part of society or of individuals. We particularly deplore that section of the press that every so often takes up the question once again with the obvious intention of confusing good people and drawing them into error with misleading evidence, questionable polls, and even falsified statements from some cleric or other.

OBEDIENCE TO NATURE'S LAWS

On the part of Catholics, We must urge the wide dissemination of the principle, firmly founded on truth, that the only way to protect the physical and moral health of the family and of society is through whole-hearted obedience to the laws of nature, or rather of the Creator, and most of all by fostering a sacred, heart-felt respect for them.

In this matter, everything depends on the intention. You can multiply laws and make the penalties heavier; you can give irrefutable proofs of the stupidity of birth-control theories and of the harm that comes from putting them into practice; but as long as there is no sincere determination to let the Creator carry on His work as He chooses, then human selfishness will always find new sophistries and excuses to still the voice of conscience (to the extent it can), and to carry on abuses.

Now the value of the testimony offered by the parents of large families lies not only in their unequivocal and forceful rejection of any deliberate compromise between the law of God and human selfishness, but also in their readiness to accept joyfully and gratefully these priceless gifts of God—their children—in whatever number it may please Him to send them.

This kind of attitude frees married couples from oppressive anxieties and remorse, and, in the opinion of outstanding doctors, creates the ideal psychological conditions for the healthy development of children born of the marriage. For, right at the beginning of these new lives, it eliminates all those worries and disturbances that can so easily leave physical or psychological scars on the mother or child.

Apart from exceptional cases—and We have had occasion to speak of these before—nature's law is basically one of harmony, and it leads to discord and contradictions only in cases where its normal operation is upset by particular circumstances which are for the most part abnormal, or by deliberate opposition from a human will. There is no eugenics that can improve upon nature: it is good as a science only so long as it aims at gaining a profound knowledge of nature's laws and respects these laws—although in some cases it may be wise to dissuade people who suffer from serious defects from getting married (cfr. Enc. *Casti connubii,* Dec. 31, 1930.

PHYSICAL AND MORAL HEALTH

Again, good common sense has always and everywhere looked upon large families as a sign, a proof, and a source of physical health, and history makes no mistake when it points to violation and abuse of the laws governing marriage and procreation as the primary cause of the decay of peoples.

Far from being a "social malady," large families are a guarantee of the moral and physical health of a people. Virtues flourish spontaneously in homes where a baby's cries always echo from the crib, and vice is put to flight, as if it has been chased away by the childhood that is renewed there like the fresh and invigorating breath of spring.

So let the weak and selfish take their example from you; let the nation continue to be loving and grateful toward you for all the sacrifices you have taken upon yourselves to raise and educate its citizens; just as the Church is pleased with you for enabling her to offer, along with you, ever healthier and larger groups of souls to the sanctifying activity of the divine Spirit.

II

In the modern civil world a large family is usually, with good reason, looked upon as evidence of the fact that the Christian faith is being lived up to, for the selfishness that We just pointed out as the principal obstacle to an increase in the size of a family group cannot be successfully overcome without recourse to ethical and religious principles.

In recent times we have seen how so-called "demographic

politics" have failed to achieve any noteworthy results; it is easy to see why, for the individual interest will almost always win out over the collective pride and selfishness which this idea so often expresses, and the aims and methods of this policy debase the dignity of the family and the person by placing them on the same level as lower species.

THE LIGHT OF CHRISTIANITY

Only the divine and eternal light of Christianity gives full life and meaning to the family and this is so true that right from the beginning and through the whole course of its history, large families have often been considered as synonymous with Christian families.

Respect for divine laws has made them abound with life; faith in God gives parents the strength and vigor they need to face the sacrifice and self-denial demanded for the raising of their children; Christian principles guide them and help them in the hard work of education; the Christian spirit of love watches over their peace and good order, and seems to draw forth from nature and bestow the deepest family joys that belong to parents, to children, to brothers and sisters.

Even externally, a large, well-ordered family is a kind of visible shrine: the sacrament of Baptism is not an exceptional event for them but something constantly renewing the joy and grace of the Lord. The series of happy pilgrimages to the Baptismal font is not yet finished when a new one to Confirmation and first Communion begins, aglow with the same innocence. The youngest of the children will scarcely have put away his little white suit among the dearest memories of life, when the first wedding veil appears to bring parents, children, and new relatives together at the foot of the altar. More marriages, more Baptisms, more first Communions follow each other like ever-new springtimes that, in a sense, make the visits of God and of His grace to the home unending.

TRUST IN GOD

But God also visits large families with His Providence, and parents, especially those who are poor, give clear testimony to this by resting all their trust in Him when human efforts are not enough. A trust that has a solid foundation and is not in vain! Providence—to put it in human words and ideas—is not a sum total of exceptional acts of divine pity; it is the ordinary result of harmonious activity on the part of the infinite wisdom, goodness and omnipotence of the Creator. God will never refuse a means of living to those He calls into being.

The Divine Master has explicitly taught that "life is worth more than food, and the body more than clothing" (*Matt.* 6, 25). If single incidents, whether small or great, seem to contradict this, it is a sign that man has placed some obstacle in the way of divine order, or else, in exceptional cases, that God has higher plans for good; but Providence is something necessary since God is the Creator.

OVERPOPULATION

The so-called problem of overpopulation of the earth is partly real and partly unreasonably feared as an imminent castrophe for modern society; but undoubtedly the rise of this problem and the continued failure to arrive at a solution of it is not due to some mixup or inertia on the part of divine Providence, but rather to disorder on man's part—especially to his selfishness and avarice.

With the progress that has been made in technology, with the new sources of energy that are just beginning to be tapped, the earth can promise prosperity to all those who will dwell on it for a long time to come.

As for the future, who can foresee what new and unsuspected resources may be found on our planet, and what surprises may be uncovered outside of it by the wonderful scientific achievements that have just barely begun? And who can be sure that the natural rhythm of procreation will be the same in the future as it is now? Is it not possible that some law that will moderate the rhythm of expansion from within may come into play? Providence has reserved the future destiny of the world to itself.

It is strange to find that the fears of some individuals are able to change well-founded hopes for prosperity into catastrophic spectres at the very moment when science is changing what used to be considered the dreams of wild imaginations into useful realities.

So overpopulation is not a valid reason for spreading illicit birth-control practices. It is simply a pretext used by those who would justify avarice and selfishness—by those nations, for instance, who fear that the expansion of others will pose a danger to their own political position and cause a lowering of the general standard of living, or by individuals, especially those who are better off, who prefer the greatest possible enjoyment of earthly goods to the praise and merit of bringing new lives into existence. The final result is that they break the fixed and certain laws of the Creator under the pretext of correcting supposed errors on the part of His Providence.

It would be more reasonable and useful if modern society would make a more determined, universal effort to correct its own conduct, by removing the causes of hunger in the overpopulated or "depressed areas," through a more active use of modern discoveries for peaceful aims, a more open political policy of collaboration and exchange, a more far-seeing and less nationalistic economy; above all, by reacting to all suggestions of selfishness with charity, to those of avarice with a more concrete application of justice.

God is not going to ask men for an accounting of the general destiny of mankind; that is His business; but He will demand an accounting of the single acts that they have deliberately performed in accordance with or against the dictates of conscience.

As for you, parents and children of large families, keep on giving a serene and firm testimony of your trust in divine Providence, and be assured that He will not fail to repay you with the testimony of His daily help and, whenever necessary, with those extraordinary helps that many of you have been happy to experience already.

III

And now a few words on your third testimony—words that may give new strength to those who are fearful and bring you a little comfort.

Large families are the most splendid flower-beds in the garden of the Church; happiness flowers in them and sanctity ripens in favorable soil. Every family group, even the smallest, was meant by God to be an oasis of spiritual peace. But there is a tremendous difference: where the number of children is not much more than one, that serene intimacy that gives value to life has a touch of melancholy or of pallor about it; it does not last as long, it may be more uncertain, it is often clouded by secret fears and remorse.

HAPPINESS IN A LARGE FAMILY

It is very different from the serenity of spirit to be found in parents who are surrounded by a rich abundance of young lives. The joy that comes from the plentiful blessings of God breaks out in a thousand different ways and there is no fear that it will end. The brows of these fathers and mothers may be burdened with cares, but there is never a trace of that inner shadow that betrays anxiety of conscience or fear of an irreparable return to loneliness. Their youth never seems to fade away, as long as the sweet fragrance of a crib remains in the home, as long as the walls of the house echo to the silvery voices of children and grandchildren.

Their heavy labors multiplied many times over, their redoubled sacrifices and their renunciation of costly amusements are generously rewarded even here below by the inexhaustible treasury of affection and tender hopes that dwell in their hearts without ever tiring them or bothering them.

And the hopes soon become a reality when the eldest daughter begins to help her mother to take care of the baby and on the day the oldest son comes home with his face beaming with the first salary he has earned himself. That day will be a particularly happy one for parents, for it will make the spectre of an old age spent in misery disappear, and they will feel assured of a reward for their sacrifices.

When there are many children, the youngsters are spared the boredom of loneliness and the discomfort of having to live in

the midst of adults all the time. It is true that they may sometimes become so lively as to get on your nerves, and their dis-
agreements may seem like small riots; but even their arguments
play an effective role in the formation of character, as long as
they are brief and superficial. Children in large families learn
almost automatically to be careful of what they do and to assume
responsibility for it, to have a respect for each other and help
each other, to be open-hearted and generous. For them, the family is a little proving-ground, before they move into the world
outside, which will be harder on them and more demanding.

VOCATIONS

All of these precious benefits will be more solid and permanent, more intense and more fruitful if the large family takes the
supernatural spirit of the Gospel, which spiritualizes everything
and makes it eternal, as its own particular guiding rule and basis.
Experience shows that in these cases, God often goes beyond the
ordinary gifts of Providence, such as joy and peace, to bestow
on it a special call—a vocation to the priesthood, to the religious
life, to the highest sanctity.

With good reason, it has often been pointed out that large
families have been in the forefront as the cradles of saints. We
might cite, among others, the family of St. Louis, the King of
France, made up of ten children, that of St. Catherine of Siena
who came from a family of twenty-five, St. Robert Bellarmine
from a family of twelve, and St. Pius X from a family of ten.

Every vocation is a secret of Providence; but these cases
prove that a large number of children does not prevent parents
from giving them an outstanding and perfect upbringing; and
they show that the number does not work out to the disadvantage

of their quality, with regard to either physical or spiritual values.

VIGILANCE AND ACTION

One last word to you, Directors and Representatives of the Associations for Large Families of Rome and of Italy.

Be careful to imprint the seal of an ever more vigilant and fruitful dynamism on the action that you intend to carry out in behalf of the dignity of large families and for their economic protection.

With regard to the first of these aims, keep in line with the directives of the Church; with regard to the second, you have to shake out of its lethargy that part of society that is not yet aware of its social responsibilities. Providence is a divine truth and reality, but it chooses to make use of human cooperators. Ordinarily it moves into action and comes to our aid when it has been summoned and practically led by the hand by man; it loves to lie hidden behind human activity. While it is only right to acknowledge that Italian legislation can legitimately boast of being most advanced in this area of affording protection to families and especially to large families, We should not close our eyes to the fact that there are still a considerable number of them who are tossed back and forth between discomfort and real privation, through no fault of their own. Your action must aim at bringing these people the protection of the laws, and in more urgent cases the help of charity. Every positive achievement in this field is like a solid stone set into the structure of the nation and of the Church; it is the very best thing you can do as Catholics and as citizens.

Calling down the divine protection upon your families and those of all Italy, placing them once again under the heavenly protection of the Holy Family of Jesus, Mary and Joseph, We impart to you with all Our heart Our paternal Apostolic Blessing.

INDISCREET ZEAL FOR NEW SOLUTIONS

Another solution is envisaged, namely sterilization, whether of the person, or simply of the action. For biological and eugenic reasons these two methods are now viewed with increasing favor and are being spread more widely by reason of new drugs which are growing in effectiveness and convenience. The reaction of certain groups of theologians to this state of affairs is symptomatic and somewhat alarming. It reveals a deviation in moral judgment which goes hand in hand with an exaggerated promptness to revise commonly received positions in favor of new techniques. This attitude proceeds from a laudable intention which, in order to help those who are in difficulty, refuses to exclude too summarily new possibilities of solution.

But the effort of adaptation is here applied in an unfortunate manner, because certain principles have been badly understood, or they have been given a meaning and a scope which cannot be theirs. The Holy See then finds itself in a situation similar to that in which Blessed Innocent XI was: more than once he found himself obliged to condemn theses advanced by moral theologians who were animated by an indiscreet zeal and an ill-judged boldness.

ANOVULANT PILLS

These principles allow us also to resolve a question much discussed today by physicians and moralists: is it lawful to prevent ovulation by means of pills employed as remedies against exaggerated reactions of the uterus and the organism, although this medication, in preventing ovulation, also renders fecundation impossible? Is it permissible for the married woman who, in spite of this temporary sterility, wishes to have relations with her husband?

The response depends upon the intention of the person. If the woman takes this medication not with a view to preventing conception, but solely on the advice of her physician, as a necessary remedy because of a uterine or organic disorder, she brings about an indirect sterilization which remains licit according to the general principle of "actions with a double effect." But a direct—and therefore an illicit—sterilization is brought about when ovulation is arrested in order to preserve the uterus and the organism from the effects of a pregnancy which it is not capable of bearing. Certain moralists hold that it is lawful to take medication with this end in view, but wrongly. It is also necessary to reject the opinion of several physicians and moralists who permit the use of these remedies when medical indications render undesirable a conception in the near future, or in other similar cases which it would not be possible to mention here: in these cases the use of medication has as its end to prevent conception by impeding ovulation; therefore, we are here dealing with direct sterilization. [Allocution to members of the Seventh Congress on Hematology. 9/12/58. Excerpts.]

4. John XXIII

Pope John was given the strength to accomplish prodigies of work for the Mystical Body in the few years allotted to his papacy. He was keenly aware of the dangers threatening dearly loved family life, and he characterized the peril as "more insistent, more seductive, and more subtle than in the past."

FAMILY FIDELITY TO GOD'S LAW

And in the light of Nazareth, Our mind searches out with special anxiety those numerous families which, because of their fidelity to the law of God not infrequently meet with sufferings and privations the like of which are unknown or little reckoned by others. We think likewise of those families which, through lack of means of employment or of health, live in constant and anxious distress. For all these suffering children and also for the more secure and serene families (whom we urge to help those others with Christian solicitude) Our fervent prayers ascend to Jesus, Mary and Joseph that the fulness of both heavenly grace and earthly consolation be poured out over them all. [To the family Front. 1/11/59. Excerpt.]

DEFECTIVE MORAL TEACHING

The levity with which on so many occasions the subject of marriage is treated, and the frightening weakening of moral standards, are caused not only by defective religious instruction—as We have pointed out—but still more by the lack of clear and precise ideas on the part of those who, by their profession, ought to be the light and guide of the young. By the vacillation of their convictions, the superficiality and even the errors of their philosophical and religious foundation, and—We say it with sorrow—sometimes even by their perverse will in opposing the action of the Church, they aim the first blow at the firmness of many consciences, for whom the encounter with anti-Christian educators and physicians stands often as the occasion and the cause of a sad apostasy.

GOD'S FECUNDITY REFLECTED IN THE FAMILY

The interior and eternal fecundity which is in the bosom of God is, in a certain way, reflected beneficent and active in the sons of men, elevated as they are to the very high dignity and duty of procreators.

In the family is to be seen the marvelous and very close cooperation of man with God: two human persons, created to the divine image and likeness, are called not only to the great mission of continuing and prolonging the creative work, in giving physical life to new beings in whom the life-giving Spirit infuses the powerful principle of immortal life; but also the more noble office which perfects the first: the civil and Christian education of their offspring.

Educators and pastors of souls know by experience what vigor of holy enthusiasm and of joyful gratitude to God such considerations raise in the hearts of the young who are preparing themselves for matrimony, and what touching seriousness of assent and of purpose are roused in their generous souls.

Therefore, let all these means be used with a joyous consciousness of the august nobility of man, of the father and the mother of the family as the first collaborators of God in the prosecution of his work in the world, in giving new members to the Mystical

Body of Christ, in peopling heaven with the elect who will sing forever the glory of the Lord. [Allocution to Prelates of the Sacred Rota. 10/25/60. Excerpts.]

We know the kind of difficulties and dangers that Christian families meet along the way. In the spiritual order, in particular, the effort of sacrifice and self-denial that is required of fathers and mothers to raise their children in a Christian way; to remain faithful to God's unchanging law in the midst of the wiles and attractions of a worldly atmosphere and mentality whose tendency is all toward pleasure and enjoyment; to build the strong rampart of a sound moral conscience and defend it against the kind of compromise and surrender that you can see here and there. Nor are we blind to anxieties in the material order that come from the straightened circumstances in which many families have to live, especially large ones and those belonging to men who are unemployed or not steadily employed or who are otherwise in need . . . (We will) encourage authorities to do something about meeting these spiritual and temporal needs . . . and keep on urging everyone, especially those who are in a comfortable position, to outdo themselves in generosity. [Feast of the Holy Family. 1/8/61. Excerpt.]

Population Increase and Economic Development

A STATEMENT OF THE PROBLEM

How can economic development and the supply of food keep pace with the continual rise in population? This is a question which constantly obtrudes itself today—a world problem, as well as one for the poverty-stricken nations.

As a world problem, the case is put thus: According to sufficiently reliable statistics the next few decades will see a very great increase in human population, whereas economic development will proceed at a slower rate. Hence, we are told, if nothing is done to check this rise in population, the world will be faced in the not too distant future with an increasing shortage in the necessities of life.

As it affects the less developed countries, the problem is stated thus: The resources of modern hygiene and medicine will very shortly bring about a notable decrease in the mortality rate, especially among infants, while the birth rate—which in such countries is unusually high—will tend to remain more or less constant, at least for a considerable period. The excess of births over deaths will therefore show a steep rise, whereas there will be no corresponding increase in the productive efficiency of the economy. Accordingly, the standard of living in these poorer countries cannot possibly improve. It must surely worsen, even to the point of extreme hardship. Hence there are those who hold the opinion that, in order to prevent a serious crisis from developing, the conception and birth of children should be secretly avoided, or in any event, curbed in some way.

THE PROBLEM EXAMINED

Truth to tell, we do not seem to be faced with any immediate or imminent world problem arising from the disproportion between the increase of population and the supply of food. Arguments to this effect are based on such unreliable and controversial data that they can only be of very uncertain validity.

Besides, the resources which God in His goodness and wisdom has implanted in Nature are well-nigh inexhaustible, and He has at the same time given man the intelligence to discover ways and means of exploiting these resources for his own advantage and his own livelihood. Hence, the real solution of the problem is not to be found in expedients which offend against the divinely established moral order and which attack human life at its very source, but in a renewed scientific and technical effort on man's part to deepen and extend his dominion over Nature. The progress of science and technology that has already been achieved opens up almost limitless horizons in this field.

As for the problems which face the poorer nations in various parts of the world, we realize, of course, that these are very real. They are caused, more often than not, by a deficient economic and social organization, which does not offer living conditions proportionate to the increase in population. They are caused, also, by the lack of effective solidarity among such peoples.

But granting this, We must nevertheless state most emphatically that no statement of the problem and no solution to it is acceptable which does violence to man's essential dignity; those

who propose such solutions base them on an utterly material-
istic conception of man himself and his life.

ONLY POSSIBLE SOLUTION

The only possible solution to this question is one which envisages the social and economic progress both of individuals and of
the whole of human society, and which respects and promotes
true human values. First consideration must obviously be given
to those values which concern man's dignity generally, and the
immense worth of each individual human life. Attention must
then be turned to the need for worldwide co-operation among
men, with a view to a fruitful and well-regulated interchange
of useful knowledge, capital and manpower.

RESPECT FOR THE LAWS OF LIFE

We must solemnly proclaim that human life is transmitted by
means of the family, and the family is based upon a marriage
which is one and indissoluble and, with respect to Christians,
raised to the dignity of a sacrament. The transmission of human
life is the result of a personal and conscious act, and, as such, is
subject to the all-holy, inviolable and immutable laws of God,
which no man may ignore or disobey. He is not therefore permitted to use certain ways and means which are allowable in
the propagation of plant and animal life.

Human life is sacred—all men must recognize that fact. From
its very inception it reveals the creating hand of God. Those
who violate His laws not only offend the divine majesty and de-
grade themselves and humanity, they also sap the vitality of the
political community of which they are members.

EDUCATION TOWARD SENSE OF RESPONSIBILITY

It is of the utmost importance that parents exercise their right and obligation toward the younger generation by securing for their children a sound cultural and religious formation. They must also educate them to a deep sense of responsibility in life, especially in such matters as concern the foundation of a family and the procreation and education of children. They must instill in them an unshakable confidence in Divine Providence and a determination to accept the inescapable sacrifices and hardships involved in so noble and important a task as the co-operation with God in the transmitting of human life and the bringing up of children.

To the attainment of this end nothing can be more effective than those principles and that supernatural aid which the Church supplies. On this score alone the right of the Church to full liberty in the exercise of her mission must be recognized.

SCIENCE IN THE SERVICE OF LIFE

Genesis relates how God gave two commandments to our first parents: to transmit human life—"Increase and multiply"— and to bring nature into their service—"Fill the earth, and sub-due it." These two commandments are complementary.

Nothing is said in the second of these commandments about destroying nature. On the contrary, it must be brought into the service of human life.

We are sick at heart, therefore, when We observe the contra-diction which has beguiled so much modern thinking. On the one hand we are shown the fearful specter of want and misery which threatens to extinguish human life, and on the other hand we find scientific discoveries, technical inventions and economic resources being used to provide terrible instruments of ruin and death.

A provident God grants sufficient means to the human race to find a dignified solution to the problems attendant upon the transmission of human life. But these problems can become difficult of solution, or even insoluble, if man, led astray in mind and perverted in will, turns to such means as are opposed to right reason, and seeks ends that are contrary to his social nature and the intentions of Providence.

But We must remind you here of an important truth: the Christian conception of life demands of all—whether highborn or lowly—a spirit of moderation and sacrifice. That is what God calls us to by His grace.

There is, alas, a spirit of hedonism abroad today which beguiles men into thinking that life is nothing more than the quest for pleasure and the satisfaction of human passions. This attitude is disastrous. Its evil effects on soul and body are undeniable. Even on the natural level temperance and simplicity of life are the dictates of sound policy. On the supernatural level, the Gospels and the whole ascetic tradition of the Church require a sense of mortification and penance which assures the rule of the spirit over the flesh, and offers an efficacious means of expiating the punishment due to sin, from which no one, except Jesus Christ and His Immaculate Mother, is exempt. [Mater et Magistra Encyclical. 5/15/61. Excerpts.]

5. *Pope Paul VI*

Pope Paul's reign seems hardly to have begun and yet he has already made several reaffirmations of Christian conjugal morality. When he was still Monsignor Montini, he sent messages to Cardinal Siri for the annual Social Week of Italian Catholics; these referred to the attacks on new life and spoke of the "fraud" against the plans of the Creator. One day, hopefully, Christians will be able to consult many additional documents of Pope Paul on marriage and find therein, as they will find here, the unchanging voice of their Good Shepherd.

POPULATION AND ECONOMICS

Following a praiseworthy tradition, the well-deserving organizers of Italian Catholic Social Weeks have again this year expressed to His Holiness their desire that His blessing should descend upon the work of the forthcoming session at Palermo, to be as always a pledge of heavenly light and comfort.

I have the honor to inform Your Eminence that the Holy Father has most willingly deigned to accept this filial request, all the more so since the subject proposed this year merits in many ways the most attentive consideration.

It is, in fact, proposed to examine, with the guidance of the Church's teaching, the vexed question of population, with especial regard to the relations between population increase and economic development, to determine the causes which upset the equilibrium between these two phenomena and to indicate possible remedies.

There is, in truth, nothing more important to society than these delicate problems. At the same time, it is easy to discern the Church's vital interest in their just solution. From this solution derive consequences closely linked with the transmission of human life and thereby affecting also the family, the mother cell of society, which the Church expects to give her members their earliest training.

The problem, then, is not a purely economic one, but has also, especially for Catholics, a moral and religious character. Moreover, when considered on a universal scale, it affects particularly international relations, since it entails the finding of remedies for a disorder which arises not so much from nature as from the wills of men, and the re-establishment in those zones burdened by over-population of just harmony between demographic density and vital resources. In consequence, this question is linked with the fundamental problem of peace, which as St. Augustine testifies, is precisely "the tranquility of order," by virtue of which each State can carry out its social mission and make its contribution to the welfare of the international community.

POPULATION DISTRIBUTION

It was to this world peace, attainable through a better balance between men and their means of subsistence, that the present Pontiff referred, when, on Pentecost Sunday 1941, at the height of the World War, He expressed His desire to cooperate "in the future organization of that new order for which the world is waiting amidst the furious ferment of this present struggle." To achieve this aim, He expressed hopes for a "more favorable distribution of population upon the surface of the earth . . . . that surface which God created and prepared for the use of all."

Everybody will admit that the far-seeing paternal solicitude of the Sovereign Pontiff has now become more urgent than ever, since the statistics of recent years—in spite of the truly bound-less natural resources of the earth—show an acute disproportion in many parts of the world between population and food sup-plies. This fact, while it has justly claimed the attention of statesmen and rulers, has nevertheless created in many circles an atmosphere of apprehension at humanity's continuous popu-lation increase, which leads some to believe that the only solu-tion possible is that of the limitation of births. Hence derives the revival of neo-malthusian propaganda against the very sources of life, a propaganda which, in the name of false scien-tific presuppositions, spreads ever more widely ideas and habits that ominously undermine public morality, and lead society toward an ever more serious and more baneful weakening of moral and religious principles.

Catholics, being aware of the social needs and duties sur-rounding them, will consequently feel the impelling necessity of finding the safe road in this field also, even in the difficult circumstances of the present time, where there will arise perfect harmony between economic postulates and Christian principles. The latest providential encounter of thought and action occa-sioned by the Social Week of Palermo, will therefore, offer a favorable opportunity for Italian Catholics to make their effica-cious contribution in this field, since the theme proposed will there be considered—according to the program—under a fourfold aspect: metaphysical-moral, medico-biological, economic and political.

In order that the discussion of such a delicate theme may lead to useful results, it will help the speakers of the Congress to reflect upon certain teachings of the Church's Magisterium which must guide and illuminate them in their labors.

First of all, they will remember that no solution of the problem of population can ever be considered just and true unless it takes into due account the sacred and inviolable value of human life, and unless it avoids in any way disregarding the laws governing its proper transmission. That transmission finds its natural application in the precincts of the family and in the dignity of conjugal relations; it embraces both the procreation and education of offspring.

DEFRAUDING NATURE'S INTENTIONS

Every attempt on life during its progress from the parents to the cradle is therefore a crime, which is absolutely unjustifiable for any reasons of State or on eugenic or economic pretexts. Such attempts include not only the direct killing of the innocent but also any defrauding of nature's intentions, which, as such, express the will of the Creator Himself.

"If a profound understanding of the common good is the soul of a healthy and strong State," the Holy Father warned in His radio address to the Swiss people on September 20, 1946, "then the dignity and the holiness of married life and family life are, as it were, its backbone. When, therefore, this latter is gravely wounded, the State's strength is finished and its people fall sooner or later in ruin." For this reason, when addressing midwives, He inculcated "the apostolate of appreciation and love for the life that is being born" and defined as being "opposed to the mind of God and to the words of Sacred Scripture, and, for that matter, to sound reason and to the sentiments of nature" (Discourse of Oct. 29, 1951) that modern mentality which is hostile to the ideal of a numerous family.

It is also necessary to keep in mind another teaching which is similarly fundamental, when examining the knotty problem of overpopulation. It is the imperative necessity "that those goods created by God for all men should be equitable shared in by all, according to the principles of justice and charity" (Encyclical 'Sertum Laetitiae'), This doctrine, reaffirmed by the Holy Father in the Pentecost radio address already referred to, while recognizing every individual's right of access to the primordial goods, also establishes in international relations the equally natural obligation of social justice, which binds more wealthy peoples to assist those countries less well provided.

"In the field of a new order based on moral principles," His Holiness declared in the above-mentioned document, "there is no room for narrow, selfish calculations which tend to take over the economic sources of those materials of common use in such a way that nations less favored by nature are cut off from them." It follows that a really adequate study of the relations between population density and means of subsistence must tend to take place on a world-wide scale, while the problem to which they give rise cannot be solved except on that same scale, through the industrious solidarity of all peoples in such a manner that, those artificial barriers which divide them being removed, there may arise a more orderly circulation of peoples, of capital and of material goods.

SATISFYING THE NEEDS OF ALL

With this subordination of particular national economic welfare to the common good of the society of nations, frontiers will no longer be valleys which divide but bridges which unite, and material goods will be free to fulfill their natural function of satisfying the needs of all.

It was to this very union that the Sovereign Pontiff ardently exhorted all when He said, in His Christmas radio address in 1952: "Let every nation develop its own potentialities in regard to living standards and employment, and contribute to a corresponding progress of nations less favored. Although even the most perfect realization of international solidarity would hardly bring about perfect equality among nations, still, there is an urgent need that this solidarity be put into practice at least enough to change perceptibly the present situation." On the other hand, the world's natural resources, offering as they do immense possibilities of exploitation, and the prospect which human intelligence and labor open up for the future, are very far from justifying the gloomy predictions of the prophets of neo-malthusianism. If this or that region is still burdened with overpopulation, it would be wrong, the Holy Father goes on, "to blame the natural law for the present miseries of the world, when it is clear that these derive from the lack of mutual solidarity of men and peoples."

Efforts to re-establish the equilibrium between growing population and means of livelihood are therefore not to be directed toward violation of the laws of life or interference with the natural flux and flow of the human family. Such an attitude of renouncement of life, indeed, kills the noblest aspirations of the spirit; while a declining birth-rate, aimed at by such systems, has always proved sooner or later to be, in the history of the nations, a sign of defeat and of doom. No, such efforts must rather tend to educate men's consciences regarding the value and responsibility of human life, to foster a more equitable distribution of the world's goods, to exploit natural resources in an ever more rational manner, to protect the family in all that concerns its inviolable rights and the exercise of its high function.

At the same time, these efforts must avoid having recourse to those defensive and eugenic measures, recently denounced by His Holiness in His address to specialists in genetics, which impair the freedom and dignity of the human person and which "moral commonsense and especially Christian morals must reject both in principle and in practice" (Osservatore Romano Sept. 9, 1953). Nor must we forget, in this respect, as the Holy Father has so often repeated, the advantages which may be had by favoring the flow of migration toward regions which are not yet sufficiently utilized, and thus alleviating the serious burden of unemployment.

MUTUAL BENEFITS

In His address of June 1, 1941, the Holy Father said: "If the two parties, namely those who decide to leave their native soil and those who admit the newcomers, remain loyally solicitous for the elimination of everything which would impede the growth and development of true confidence between the country of emigration and that of immigration, all those sharing in this change of places and persons will benefit by it: the families will receive a piece of ground which will be a fatherland for them in the true sense of the word; countries of dense population will as a result be relieved and their peoples will create new friendships for themselves in strange lands; and the states which receive the emigrants will gain industrious citizens."

The sessions of the forthcoming Congress will concentrate on enlightening the consciences of Catholics regarding such lofty obligations, and on promoting an ever more profound study of these problems, in order to give a solid training to persons engaged in this field of activity; and from this Congress the Holy Father hopes for most flattering results.

May the voice of such an elect assembly make itself heard in salutary warning amidst the many distressing ideologies of the present day; and may it serve as a safe guide to many, in a world which is prone to ignore the requirements of ethics and supernatural ideals, and which therefore has all the greater need of being strongly reminded of the supreme and irreplaceable values of the Catholic Faith!

It is as a pledge of this that the Holy Father cordially imparts to Your Eminence, to the organizers and lecturers, and to all those attending the Social Week in Palermo, His Apostolic Benediction. [Msgr. Montini to Cardinal Siri, XXVI Social Week of Italian Catholics. 9/28/53.]

RESPONSIBILITY TO KNOW

It is sufficient to call to mind the tendency of some to recur to fraud in order to evade those laws which so well defend family stability; of others to have recourse to the spreading of neo-malthusian practices which violate the divine laws governing the transmission of life; of others still, and of certain elements of the press, who publish public scandals which deaden that one and indissoluble, faithful and fruitful married love. To this may be added the uneasy economic conditions of modern life, which, more or less common to every country, are also causing modifications of a social and ethical character even in Italy and giving rise to new and complex family problems which require on the part of Catholics no longer only a general respect for the family and a vague knowledge of its traditional prerogatives. [Msgr. Montini to Cardinal Siri XXVII Social Week of Italian Catholics. 9/19/54.]

DECREASED FERTILITY

Unfortunately, there is another negative phenomenon: decreased fertility in the modern family. There are various causes for it, not all of them immoral. Fruitfulness requires a family that is healthy, strong, united, protected, considerate. These words do not often characterize the modern family. But unfortunately there is no doubt that widely diffused, dangerous doctrines also contribute to limiting the family's growth, doctrines at everyone's doorstep. Almost always they are presented in inexact terms while covering themselves with scientific appearances. We refer primarily to neo-malthusianism and birth control.

It is a disgrace and a misfortune, but two capital sins of modern immorality follow upon these principles: The vicious practice of contraception (onanism) and the criminal suppression of the new life germinating in the womb (abortion).

As everyone knows there is an immense volume of literature and casuistry focusing on the morality of these questions. For our purpose it is enough to note that it is difficult to calculate the extension of these sins. Those who know something about the matter give frightening figures.

We are faced with moral deviance and crimes which offend God's design for the transmission of life. They cast a shadow of infamy across our civilization. We are faced with personal crimes which become social crimes. Perhaps not even the devastating plagues of ancient and medieval civilizations were as disastrous as this systematic corrosion of our nations' vitality. Perhaps wars take away fewer human lives than this cold suppression of humanity, of beings called into life and into death by their own parents.

EGOISM, THE SCOURGE WHICH DEPRESSES AND DISSOLVES THE FAMILY

Perhaps this scourge has a name, very generic but in this case tragically true: *egoism*. If egoism limits the rule of human love, it debases, depresses and dissolves the family. The art of loving is not as easy as commonly believed. Instinct is an insufficient teacher, much less passion or pleasure.

Love can terminate in two contrary expressions: egoism and sacrifice. The first tends to cut off life; the second to make a gift of it. Christ Himself has said it: "He who would save his life will lose it; but he who loses his life—*propter me*—(that is, according to the law of Christ) will find it" (Matt. 16:25).

Conjugal union has the love of Christ for its fundamental model. Christ sacrifices Himself for mankind, redeems it, and from it composes His Church by the supreme giving of Himself. Whoever forsakes these divine footsteps directs his love toward sterility and the cruel fear of new life.

CONTROLLING THE FRUITFULNESS OF MATRIMONY

Another serious problem of family morality, related to the previous one, is the control of matrimony's fruitfulness. This becomes a vexing problem when a family does not have the means of giving new birth a healthy start in life, when (as so often happens) there is not sufficient food.

We refer this delicate question also to the prudent consideration of those who are competent. Here we only touch upon it to remind you that any act, willfully malicious, which tends to deprive the conjugal union of its natural reproductive power is gravely culpable. This is an especially demanding element of God's law. Married couples should not forget it, nor should those who devote themselves to maintaining health or to instructing the spirit.

We must also remind you: Although married couples can with caution have recourse to methods, licit in themselves, which they understand will avoid the fruitfulness of matrimony, their caution should not proceed from a previously determined and fixed will nor can it be without true and well founded motives. The teaching of Pius XII on this point is very steady and it can provide orientation.

But we should ask ourselves: is there not too much concern these days about this question; does it not tend to favor the limitation of births rather than their regular and blessed occurrence? We should give preference to the latter, not the former.

Very often egoism tries to justify motives in favor of limitation, for egoism extinguishes life, fruitfulness, love. We wish that among Catholics the family would preserve its generous fruitfulness as much as possible. We wish that *numerous children* (Cardinal Montini's emphasis) would testify to the virtue of parents, ministers of life; to their fidelity, their love, their confidence in Providence, their affection for their children. And we wish that society would provide approval and assistance, as much as needed.

CONTINENCE

When the control of fertility is necessary (we may presume that in any marriage circumstances could call for it), *continence* should be the normal means of achieving it. Continence is a virtue not contrary to a couple's happiness, to the vitality of their love or of their life together. But it requires an educating; it requires moral and spiritual effort; it requires, as always, the help of prayer and grace. Continence belongs to the great program of Christian life.

Blessed are those who will impose this virtuous exercise on themselves and who will experience its hidden spiritual rewards.

[Lenten pastoral letter of Cardinal Montini—*Per la famiglia cristiana,* 1960 Excerpts.]

Those contracting marriage should not approach it superficially as a caprice of the senses, or an adventure, or an uncertain experiment, but should be conscious of the step they are taking and should see it as the great sacrament which consecrates them to the sublime mission of collaborating with God in giving life to new creatures and caring for their development with prudence and an awareness of their responsibility. [Pope Paul VI to Sacred Rota. 12/12/63.]

One who studies this unforgettable and threatening problem (hunger) is sometimes tempted to have recourse to remedies which must be regarded as worse than the problem itself, if they consist in attacking the very fecundity of life by means which human and Christian ethics must condemn as illicit.

Instead of increasing the supply of bread on the dining table of this hunger-ridden world, as modern techniques of production can do today, some are thinking in terms of diminishing by illicit means the number of those who eat with them. This is unworthy of civilization.

We know that the problem of demographic growth when unaccompanied by sufficient means of sustenance is very grave and complex. But it cannot be admitted that the solution to this problem consists in the use of methods contrary to divine law and to the sacred respect that is due to both marriage and new-born **life.** [Christmas Message to the World—1963. Excerpts.]

A RADIANT CROWN IN HEAVEN

Dear Sons and Daughters, Our heart opens to the greetings of all the families whose fecundity, crowned by a magnificent flourishing of children, is a clear demonstration of a lofty and courageous concept of the family and of a lived and conscious Faith.

You look for a word of praise and encouragement from the humble Vicar of Jesus Christ; and how can he fail to give it to you? He knows so well your situation in society, the difficulties and trials confronting you, the aspirations and ideals that impel you. Your presence in the world is a testimonial of faith, of courage, of optimism. It is an act of living, total confidence in the Providence of God. It is an eloquent demonstration of the high and holy values of the family. It is a witness to upright conscience in a society which at the present moment shows disturbing symptoms of selfishness, of indifference, of a miserable hedonism that often runs to moral depravity.

You have a great and complicated function to perform. Along with your other praiseworthy initiatives, you are upholding the institution of the family, in the sacred and inviolate integrity of the bonds of affection and of duty that hold it together. It is yours to honor the family in its primary purpose, which is to be a wellspring, blessed and fruitful, of human life. It is yours to bring aid to the homes where the size of the family calls for special care and for social security, and to propose to government special forms of legislation to reinforce the cell of society in its organic and natural cohesion, and in the achievement of its educational mission.

That mission is to give to society and prove the worth of exemplary families, in which the very number of the children conduces to the practice of human and Christian virtues of the highest value. Families such as these often become a profound and admirable expression of mutual love, of religious piety, of incomparable affection and pure happiness.

So we do not hesitate to compare your activity, in modern society, with the leaven of the gospel parable which, though it seems little and insignificant, causes the mass to ferment (Matt. xiii, 33), pervading the whole and making it rise. We wish, therefore, to express to you our fatherly sympathy, and to encourage you to go forward with your little ones with unflagging confidence in the way you are traveling—a way often rough and difficult, but blessed with great satisfactions even humanly speaking, and above all with a wealth of heavenly graces which prepare for you a radiant crown in Heaven.

Courage, dear sons and daughters. We are near you with our daily prayer. May the Lord be always at your side with his most tender and provident love, sustaining you in the fulfilment of your duties as educators and moulders of consciences. May He aid you to overcome your trials, and comfort you always, in every hour of your life.

And while invoking upon you the continuous gifts of His peace, we impart upon all of you here present, your dear ones, your associations and all large families, our propitiatory apostolic blessing. [Address to Association of Large Families. 12/15/63.]

6. *Explosion or Backfire*

Statement of the Catholic Bishops of the United States

November, 1959

For the past several years a campaign of propaganda has been gaining momentum to influence international, national, and personal opinion in favor of birth prevention programs. The vehicle for this propaganda is the recently coined terror technique phrase, "population explosion." The phrase, indeed, alerts all to the attention that must be given to population pressures, but it also provides a smoke screen behind which a moral evil may be foisted on the public and for obscuring the many factors that must be considered in this vital question.

More alarming is the present attempt of some representatives of Christian bodies who endeavor to elaborate the plan into a theological doctrine which envisages artificial birth prevention within the married state as the "will of God." Strangely too, simply because of these efforts and with callous disregard of the thinking of hundreds of millions of Christians and others who reject the position, some international and national figures have made the statement that artificial birth prevention within the married state is gradually becoming acceptable even in the Catholic Church. This is simply not true.

The perennial teaching of the Catholic Church has distinguished artificial birth prevention, which is a frustration of the marital act, from other forms of control of birth which are morally permissible. Method alone, however, is not the only question involved. Equally important is the sincere and objective examination of the motives and intentions of the couples involved, in view of the nature of the marriage contract itself. As long as due recognition is not given to those fundamental questions, there can be no genuine understanding of the problem.

At the present time, too, there is abundant evidence of a systematic, concerted effort to convince United States' public opinion, legislators and policy makers that United States national agencies, as well as international bodies, should provide with public funds and support, assistance in promoting artificial birth prevention for economically under-developed countries. The alleged purpose, as already remarked, is to prevent a hypothetical "population explosion." Experts, however, have not yet reached agreement on the exact meaning of the phrase. It is still a hypothesis that must stand the test of science. Yet, pessimistic population predictors seizing on the popular acceptence of the phrase, take little account of economic, social and cultural factors and changes. Moreover, it would seem that if the predictors of population explosion wish to avail themselves to the right to foretell *population increases*, they must concede the right to predict *production increases* of food as well as of employment and educational opportunities.

The position of United States Catholics to the growing and needy population of the world is a realistic one which is grounded in the natural law (which, it should be made clear, is not the law of the jungle, as sometimes erroneously supposed) and in respect for the human person, his origin, freedom, responsibility and destiny. They believe that the goods of the earth were created by God for the use of all men and that men should not be arbitrarily tailored to fit a niggling and static image of what they are entitled to, as conceived by those who are more fortunate, greedy or lazy. The thus far hidden reservoirs of science and of the earth unquestionably will be uncovered in this era of marvels and offered to humanity by dedicated persons with faith in mankind, and not by those seeking short cuts to comfort at the expense of the heritage of their own or other peoples.

United States Catholics believe that the promotion of artificial birth prevention is a morally, humanly, psychologically and politically disastrous approach to the population problem. Not only is such an approach ineffective in its own aims, but it spurns the basis of the real solution, sustained effort in a sense of human solidarity. Catholics are prepared to dedicate themselves to this effort, already so promisingly initiated in national and international circles. *They will not, however, support any public assistance, either at home or abroad, to promote artificial birth prevention, abortion or sterilization whether through direct aid or by means of international organizations.*

The fundamental reason for this position is the well considered objection to promoting a moral evil—an objection not founded solely on any typically or exclusive Catholic doctrine, but on the natural law and on basic ethical considerations. However, quite apart from the moral issue, there are other cogent reasons why Catholics would not wish to see any official support or even favor given such specious methods of "assistance."

Man himself is the most valuable productive agent. Therefore, economic development and progress are best promoted by *creating conditions* favorable to his *highest development*. Such progress implies discipline, self-control and the disposition to postpone present satisfactions for future gains. The widespread use of contraceptives would hinder rather than promote the acquisition of these qualities needed for the social and economic changes in underdeveloped countries.

Immigration and emigration—even within the same country— have their role to play in solving the population problem. It has been said that migration to other countries is no ultimate solution because of difficulties of absorbing populations into other economies. But it is a matter of record that migration has helped as a solution. Sixty million people migrated successfully from Europe to the Americas in the last 150 years. When the nomadic Indians roamed the uncultured plains of North America before the coming of these immigrants, the entire country with its estimated Indian population of only 500,000 and its shortage of food, would have been regarded as "overpopulated" according to the norms of the exponents of Planned Parenthood. Yet, the same plains today are being retired into a "land bank" because they are overproductive in a land of 175 millions. It is, therefore, apparent that to speak of a population explosion in the United States in these circumstances is the sheerest kind of nonsense.

The Soviets in their wooing of economically underdeveloped countries do not press artificial birth prevention propaganda on them as a remedy for their ills. Rather they allure them into the communist orbit by offering education, loans, technical assistance and trade, and they boast that their economic system is able to use human beings in constructive work and to meet all their needs. The Russian delegate to the relatively recent meeting of the United Nations Economic Commission on Asia and the Far East proclaimed, "The key to progress does not lie in a limitation of population through artificial reduction of the birth rate, but in the speedy defeat of the economic backwardness of these countries." The communist record of contempt for the value of human life gives the lie to this hypocritical propaganda, but to peoples aspiring to economic development and political status, the deceit is not immediately evident. Confronted on the one hand by the prospect of achieving their goals without sacrificing natural fertility and on the other by the insistence that reducing natural fertility is essential to the achievement of such goals, how could these peoples be reasonably expected to reject communism? Yet, the prophets of "population explosion" in alleging that contraception will thwart communism naively emphasize its specious attractiveness in these areas.

United States Catholics do not wish to ignore or minimize the problem of population pressure, but they do deplore the studious omission of adequate reference to the role of modern agriculture in food production. The "population explosion" alarmists do not place in proper focus the ideal of increasing the acreage or the acreage yield to meet the food demands of an increasing population. By hysterical terrorism and bland misrepresentation of data they dismiss these ideas as requiring too much time for the development of extensive education and new distribution methods and for the elimination of apathy, greed and superstition. Such arguments merely beg the question, for the implementation of their own program demands the fulfillment of the same conditions. It seems never to dawn on them that in a chronic condition where we have more people than food, the logical answer would be, not to decrease the number of people but to increase the food supply which is almost unlimited in potential.

We make these observations to direct attention to the very real problem of population pressures. Such remarks are not intended to exhaust this complex subject, not to discourage demographers, economists, agricultural experts and political scientists in their endeavors to solve the problem. Rather our intention is to reaffirm the position of the Catholic Church that the only true solutions are those that are morally acceptable under the natural law of God. Never should we allow the unilateral "guesstimates" of special pleaders to stampede or terrorize the United States into a national or international policy inimical to human dignity. For, the adoption of the morally objectionable means advocated to forestall the so-called "population explosion" may backfire on the human race.